GW00493892

MINECRAFT

THE CRAFTER'S KITCHEN

For young chefs and their families!

MINECRAFT

THE CRAFTER'S KITCHEN

An Official Minecraft
Cookbook
FOR **YOUNG**
CHEFS AND **THEIR**
FAMILIES

Random House Worlds
New York

CONTENTS

INTRODUCTION

Whether you live in Minecraft like I do or whether you are a person living on Earth, there's something we all share: a love of good food!

Who I am? You may call me the Gourmand. Why the Gourmand? I think of myself as something of a foodie, because I like to try out new foods I find during my adventures. I've traveled all over the place you know as Minecraft, going everywhere from the plains with bee's nests and chickens to deep into the jungles with melons and cocoa to high up in the mountains with rabbits. The garden at my home gives me all sorts of fruits and vegetables. I've been a happy eater.

But then I learned about this place called Earth! Not only does Earth have all sorts of things to offer (even if it's missing important things like mooshrooms), but it also has so many more foods than I could ever have dreamed up. There I was, happily drinking my milk, having no idea you could use it to make yogurt, chocolate ice milk, cheese, and more. I was cheerfully chomping down on carrots with little pieces spraying everywhere, not realizing I could make a carrot salad.

While adventuring around Earth looking for recipes, I also learned that you can't generate a new world here like you can in Minecraft. As I've observed Earth, I've come to realize that its beautiful environments are more fragile than they might seem, so taking good care of the world is important. This book includes some tips on sustainability, which is all about not harming the world, so we can all enjoy its bounties for years to come. You can get your friends and family involved and protect your world!

But focusing on sustainability doesn't mean we can't have fun or eat wonderful foods! You know, just thinking about all these recipes is making me feel hungry. You can make every recipe with your family, snack on them while playing Minecraft, or prepare them for a birthday party. Come on, let's go exploring through these Minecraft-inspired recipes together! Bon appétit!

PLAINS

Big, flat, covered in grass. Boring? Definitely not. Plains might look basic, but they're actually incredibly rich biomes. These vast areas of mostly flat, mostly treeless grassland stretch for hundreds of miles on continents all over the world. Flocks of birds feast on the grass seeds, rivers meander through the land, and gophers, mice, and chipmunks scurry between the stems.

If you're looking for plains in central Africa, you might visit the Serengeti. These tropical grasslands are the home to millions of grazing animals like elephants and rhinos. Birds perch in the scattered trees and hippos wallow in shallow rivers.

But on the chillier steppes of Asia and Eastern Europe, you're more likely to find herds of yaks or horses running across the short grasses. No tall trees here—there's not enough rainfall.

There's nothing like a stroll through the plains on a sunny day. I can stop and smell the flowers, tame a horse or two, and of course they're a great place for farming.

I do all my own farming, but I've noticed a lot of people on Earth go to stores for their food. Kind of like trading emeralds with villagers, only the folks you buy from can say more than "Hrm."

Short grass grows on the prairies of North America as well—and so does tall grass. Native varieties like big bluestem grass grow up to eight feet! These grasses and others send down their long, tangled roots, which help to hold the soil in place.

Millions of bison used to roam the Plains states like Oklahoma, Colorado, and Kansas. They grazed on the grasses and contributed to the biome, too. The bison's small hooves are pointed. When they run and paw at the soil, their hooves punch holes in the ground. This is like aerating a lawn, allowing water and nutrients to get to the grass roots.

In the nineteenth century, European settlers slaughtered so many bison that the giant animals almost went extinct. By the late 1880s, only a few hundred wild bison were left. But people have worked to bring the bison back. They've crossbred bison with cattle and protected those that are left. More than 20,000 bison now live in herds on the Plains again.

But the Great Plains are now facing an even greater threat—climate change. The Plains states are growing hotter and hotter. Extreme heat means stress for animals, wild plants, and farmers' crops. And parts of the Plains states aren't just growing hotter. They're also growing drier. Less rainfall? More dust, less grass—and way more risk of wildfires.

Indigenous groups have taken care of the Plains land for centuries by setting ground-clearing fires. Natural wildfires, like those sparked by lightning, have been a part of the seasonal cycle for many plains. But when these fires are sparked accidentally by people or power lines and sheets of flame sweep across the grasslands, people and animals lose their homes—and sometimes, their lives.

The North American grasslands might be getting hotter and drier, but it does sometimes rain. And thanks to climate change, that rain is much more likely to be a torrent, not a drizzle. That's because the warmer air can hold even more moisture. It builds and builds and then it lets go as huge storms, which flood the dry land.

Farming can be tough on grasslands, too. Plains are great places for growing grains like oats and wheat—those crops are basically grasses topped with edible heads. North American plains have rich soil, which is great for farming. But turning grasslands into acres of crops means that animals lose their homes and food. And spraying pesticides kills the bees and other important bugs that the biome depends on.

Composting helps. When farmers add compost to their soil, it enriches the earth, which lets farmers cut down on fertilizer. Composting food scraps also helps reduce carbon emissions—10 percent of all greenhouse gas emissions are from food loss and waste!

HOW YOU CAN HELP

Start your own backyard compost pile! Done right, compost shouldn't smell at all, even with rotting food scraps buried in it.

COMPOST DOS AND DON'TS

DO compost fruits, vegetables, grass clippings, eggshells, dried leaves, wood ashes, plain bread, plain pasta, tea bags, newspapers, brown paper bags, coffee filters, hair, dryer lint, even cotton cloth like T-shirts and vacuum cleaner bags!

DO NOT compost fats and oils, like butter or cooking oil, meat, bones, dairy foods, animal poop, or charcoal. These things attract maggots, rats, and flies—and they smell!

HOW TO BUILD YOUR COMPOST PILE

Keep a container on your kitchen counter. Toss in all the compost material you use during the day. Then take it out and dump it at night. You can also buy a sealed compost container that doesn't need to be emptied for several days.

Next, think of what kind of outdoor compost container you'd like to use. You can buy big plastic composters that are shaped like a cube or a barrel. You can make an enclosure out of chicken wire. Or you can just put your compost right on the ground in a pile. That way, earthworms can help you get your compost started.

Then, start layering. All good compost has layers of "green" materials and "brown" materials. "Green" compost is food scraps and fresh plants, like fresh grass clippings. "Brown" compost is dry stuff, like dried leaves, dried grass, dirt, and dryer lint. Try for a mix of one-third green compost to two-thirds brown compost. But it doesn't really matter. You can create great compost with pretty much any mixture from the list.

If it doesn't rain much, throw some water on your compost occasionally. Turn it over with a shovel a few times and mix it up. After several months, take a look at the bottom of the pile. See dirt? You did it! Spread that beautiful fertilizer on your garden or in the soil of your houseplants and know that you did a little bit to fight climate change.

When we compost in Minecraft, we can get bone meal through it. You might not get bone meal, but you can get fertilizer of your own.

I love growing wheat and using it to make bread, cookies, and cakes. I've also used it to heal horses and make baby cows! But on Earth, there's lots more to do with wheat, like make this delicious pasta.

DIRECTIONS

1. Break the egg into a small bowl and whisk with a fork to break it up.

2. In a large bowl, mix the flour and salt. Make a well in the center large enough to hold the egg. Pour in the egg and with a fork begin to stir in the flour, pulling in a little at a time from the edges until all the flour is mixed in and the dough comes together in a ball.

3. Turn the dough out onto a lightly floured board and knead it for a good 10 minutes, until the dough is smooth. Cover with an upside-down bowl and let it rest for at least 30 minutes.

4. Now you can roll out the dough with a rolling pin as thinly as you can and cut into strips or form little shapes by hand.

HOW TO MAKE
PASTA

Once you learn how to make pasta, you can experiment with substituting other whole-grain flours for part or all of the all-purpose flour. This recipe is for one serving, and it's super easy to build on. Just multiply by the number of people you're cooking for!

Serves 1

INGREDIENTS

1 large egg
3/4 cup unbleached all-purpose flour, plus more for dusting
Pinch of salt

GNOCCHI

The traditional way to make gnocchi (pronounced "NYOH-kee") is with boiled potatoes, but here we use instant potato flakes to make ours, which is super fast and easy. Serve the gnocchi tossed with sauce, such as The Simplest Tomato Sauce (page 17). Another way to use gnocchi is to mix them with sauce and transfer them to a baking dish. Sprinkle with parmesan and/or shredded mozzarella and bake at 375°F until the cheese is bubbling and browned, about 30 minutes.

Serves 4 to 6

INGREDIENTS

1 cup instant potato flakes

1 cup boiling water

Kosher salt

1 large egg

1 cup unbleached all-purpose flour, plus more for dusting

3 tablespoons grated parmesan cheese

½ teaspoon ground white pepper

½ teaspoon ground nutmeg

I still remember the first potatoes I grew: I fought a zombie while I was building my first shelter, and it dropped a potato! I decided to plant it, so I hoed some dirt into farmland and carefully irrigated by placing water nearby. After a day or two, the potato plant was ready to harvest: it yielded five potatoes! I planted three to grow more, and the other two I baked. So simple, yet so delicious!

DIRECTIONS

1. In a large bowl, combine the potato flakes, boiling water, and 1 teaspoon kosher salt. It will be very stiff. Let cool for 10 minutes.

2. Stir the egg, flour, parmesan, white pepper, and nutmeg into the potato mixture until it comes together in a soft dough. It will be sticky. Dust a work surface with flour. Dump the dough onto the work surface and knead gently for a minute.

3. If cooking the gnocchi right away, bring a large pot of salted water to a boil.

4. Divide the dough into 8 equal pieces. Roll each piece into a rope 12 inches long. Cut the rope crosswise into 12 pieces. (You may have to dust with a bit more flour if the dough is too sticky.) The easiest way to form gnocchi is just to press your finger into each piece of dough to make a dimple. Or for the characteristic ridges, use your fingertips to press each piece of dough into the rounded (top) part of a fork and drag the dough down to the end of the tines; the dough should fold over itself and off the edge of the fork as you drag.

5. If making the gnocchi to be cooked later, spread them onto a parchment-lined baking sheet and freeze until firm; then transfer the gnocchi to a zipper storage bag and freeze. When you want to cook some, just cook them from frozen as described in the next step.

6. If cooking the gnocchi now, add them to the boiling water and cook until they float to the top of the pot, then cook 1 minute longer. Drain the gnocchi.

This one is really interesting. We don't have tomatoes in Minecraft, but I love the bright red color. It makes me think of redstone. I also wonder if it would be a good way to get red dye. I'd like to try making red dye from it, like I can with rosebushes, red tulips, beetroot, or poppies. Once this colorful recipe is done, we can add it on top of the pasta we made earlier. Is combining these things like a form of crafting?

THE SIMPLEST TOMATO SAUCE

Makes about 3 cups

INGREDIENTS

- 1/4 cup olive oil
- 1 small onion, chopped (about 1 cup)
- 3 cloves garlic, smashed and peeled
- 1 (28-ounce) can crushed tomatoes
- 1 medium carrot, for sweetness
- 1/2 cup water
- 1 teaspoon kosher salt
- 6 sprigs fresh basil (optional)

DIRECTIONS

1. In a large shallow pot, heat the olive oil over medium-high heat. Add the onion and the garlic and stir and cook until fragrant and beginning to brown, about 5 minutes.

2. Reduce the heat to a simmer and, being careful—because it will splatter—pour in the tomatoes, carrot, water, salt, and basil (if using). Give it a stir and simmer uncovered until the carrot is soft, 20 to 30 minutes. You can either mash the carrot into the sauce or remove it and have it as a cook's treat.

VARIATIONS

Latin American flavors: Add 1 teaspoon dried oregano, 1 teaspoon ground cumin, and 1 chopped jalapeño pepper along with the crushed tomatoes. A squeeze of lime would be nice at the end.

Moroccan flavors: Add 1 teaspoon ground ginger, 2 tablespoons sweet or hot paprika, and 1 1/2 teaspoons ground cumin when you're cooking the onion. Add 1/4 cup chopped fresh cilantro with the crushed tomatoes.

West African flavors: Add a chunk of grated peeled fresh ginger, 1 chopped red or green bell pepper, and 1 or 2 chopped habanero chiles when you sauté the onions. Add 1 teaspoon berbere spice with the tomatoes.

BLT PASTA SALAD

Here's a great way to use leftover cooked pasta. It's like an inside-out BLT sandwich!

Serves 4

INGREDIENTS

DRESSING
½ cup mayonnaise

⅓ cup plain yogurt

1 tablespoon grated yellow onion

2 teaspoons sugar

½ teaspoon kosher salt

¼ teaspoon freshly ground black pepper

SALAD
Kosher salt

8 ounces dried pasta or 4 recipes Fresh Pasta (page 13)

4 slices thick-cut bacon, cut into 1-inch pieces

1 pint cherry tomatoes, halved

1 small head romaine, butter, or Little Gem lettuce, roughly chopped

½ cup packaged croutons

Now here is something that's the same in both Minecraft and on Earth—we both have lots of pigs running around! Oink, oink! In Minecraft pigs will drop a porkchop, but I'm learning that on Earth there are many kinds of pig meat and different recipes people might use. (In Minecraft we have zombified piglins, but I don't want to eat any meat from those mobs.)

DIRECTIONS

1. **Make the dressing:** In a small bowl, whisk together the mayonnaise, yogurt, onion, sugar, salt, and pepper until smooth. Use right away or refrigerate for up to 2 weeks.

2. **Make the salad:** In a pot of salted boiling water, cook the pasta according to the instructions on the package. Drain in a colander and rinse with cold water.

3. In a skillet, fry the bacon over medium heat until crisp, about 5 minutes. Remove with a slotted spoon to paper towels to drain.

4. In a salad bowl, toss together the pasta, tomatoes, lettuce, and dressing. Top with the bacon and croutons.

HOW TO MAKE POTATO BREAD

All yeast doughs need to be kneaded. (Don't we all?) If this is your first time, here's how to do it. Put the ball of dough on a lightly floured work surface, like a wooden board. With both hands, push it down and away from you with the heel of your hands (the part of your palm where it meets your wrist). Rotate the dough a bit and repeat the "push down and away" motion, then continue with the push down and away and rotate sequence.

Makes one 9 × 5-inch loaf

INGREDIENTS

¾ cup hot milk

⅓ cup instant potato flakes

3 tablespoons butter, at room temperature

1½ teaspoons kosher salt

4 tablespoons sugar

½ cup warm water

1 envelope active dry yeast (2½ teaspoons)

1 large egg

1 large egg yolk

3 to 3½ cups unbleached all-purpose flour, plus more for dusting

Vegetable oil for the bowl

Cooking spray

It's pretty easy for me to craft bread, because it just takes the right amount of wheat. I also know about farming potatoes and how I can find them elsewhere, like when mobs drop them. But now I've learned you can make bread out of potatoes! This is a special sort of crafting I've never seen before. But Minecraft as a world is always expanding, so I'm ready to grow and try new things, too, even if I've never heard of them before.

DIRECTIONS

1. In a large bowl, combine the hot milk, potato flakes, butter, and salt and set aside to cool.

2. In a small bowl, combine the sugar and warm water and stir in the yeast. Let it stand for several minutes until foamy.

3. Stir the yeast mixture into the potato mixture. Stir in the whole egg and egg yolk, blending well. Now stir in enough of the flour to make a soft dough.

4. Turn the dough out onto a lightly floured board and knead it for at least 10 minutes until the dough is smooth. If you need a little extra flour that's okay; just don't be tempted to use too much or your bread will turn out tough and dry.

5. Wash out and dry the bowl you mixed the dough in and rub the inside with a little oil. Put the dough in and turn it over so the oiled side is facing up. Cover and set aside to rise until doubled in size, about 1 hour.

6. Spray a 9 × 5-inch loaf pan with cooking spray. Punch the dough down to let the air out, remove from the bowl, and pat out into a 9-inch square. Roll up into a log and place into the prepared loaf pan. Loosely cover the loaf pan with a towel and set aside to rise until doubled again, 30 to 40 minutes.

7. Preheat the oven to 350°F.

8. Bake the loaf until an instant-read thermometer inserted in the center reads 200°F, 40 to 50 minutes.

9. Remove the bread from the pan and cool on a wire rack.

Once you've made potato bread, you can turn it into burger and slider buns!

DIRECTIONS

1. Make the potato bread dough through the first rise (step 5).

2. Punch the dough down and divide into 8 equal portions for large buns or 12 portions for slider buns. Roll each portion into a ball. Press them down with your hand to flatten them a bit. Place them 2 inches apart on a large baking sheet lined with parchment paper or sprayed with cooking spray, cover them loosely, and let them rise until they have doubled in size, about 30 minutes.

3. Preheat the oven to 350°F.

4. Very gently brush the tops of the dough with the egg wash and sprinkle with the seeds (if using).

5. Bake until very nicely browned and hollow-sounding when you tap the bottoms and the internal temperature reads 200°F on an instant-read thermometer, 25 to 35 minutes.

BURGER OR SLIDER BUNS

Makes 8 burger buns or 12 slider buns

INGREDIENTS

Dough for Potato Bread (opposite)

Cooking spray (optional)

Egg wash: 1 egg beaten with 1 tablespoon water

2 tablespoons sesame or poppy seeds (optional)

Cows are mobs you see all around on the plains, mooing and hanging out. I respect the useful things they give me, like steak, milk, and leather. On Earth I see that cows are eaten for a lot more than steak, like these Sloppy Joes. No idea who these are named after, but I'd love to meet them someday! If you don't want to eat a cow, you could also use turkey meat, though turkeys are new to me. The green peppers in here remind me of emeralds, and I like to see good old familiar carrots in the recipe.

SLOPPY JOES

Serves 4

INGREDIENTS

2 tablespoons canola oil

1 medium carrot, peeled and grated

1 small onion, chopped (1 cup)

1/2 green bell pepper, chopped (2/3 cup)

2 cloves garlic, peeled and chopped

1 pound ground beef, ground turkey, or plant-based meat crumbles

1 cup tomato sauce

1/2 cup ketchup

2 tablespoons Worcestershire sauce

1 tablespoon soy sauce

1 tablespoon brown sugar

4 burger buns or 8 slider buns, store-bought or homemade (see page 21)

DIRECTIONS

1. In a large pot, heat the oil over medium-high heat until you see it shimmer. Add the carrot, onion, bell pepper, and garlic and cook and stir until the vegetables are softened and beginning to brown, about 5 minutes. Add the meat and continue to cook, breaking it up into crumbles, until the meat is no longer pink, 6 to 8 minutes.

2. Reduce the heat to a simmer and stir in the tomato sauce, ketchup, Worcestershire sauce, soy sauce, and brown sugar. Continue to cook and stir occasionally until the sauce is reduced and thickened, another 15 to 20 minutes.

3. Serve in the buns with lots of napkins. These Joes are Sloppy!

OCEANS

The boat's here! Get in—we're going for a sail. We're streaming out into the vast blue water of the ocean. Whitecaps all around us—and look! Dolphins!

Oceans, coral reefs, and estuaries—places where fresh water and ocean water mingle—make up the marine biome, the biggest biome on Earth. Our oceans cover more than 70 percent of the Earth's surface and the plants and bacteria in the waters produce more than half of the oxygen we breathe. These amazing waters provide homes to about one million animal species. The smallest animals in the world, microscopic creatures called zooplankton, live in the ocean. And the largest animal on Earth, the blue whale, calls the world's oceans home as well.

Like Minecraft world's water, Earth's ocean biome holds plenty of secrets. More than 90 percent of the ocean's species haven't even been classified, and 80 percent of the ocean is unmapped! But we do know one thing: The ocean biome is essential for life on Earth, including human life. Oceans move heat around the globe in their vast waters.

In Minecraft, I love exploring ocean monuments and underwater ruins. Sometimes I'll even bring home a sea lantern or two. But these human-made ocean structures seem a lot less fun and a lot more harmful.... I don't think I'd take any souvenirs.

They regulate the temperatures on land, keeping life on Earth from getting too hot or too cold. Humans can travel around the world on our oceans and get food and medicine from its watery depths.

Our oceans also store carbon dioxide, one of the gases that causes climate change. When carbon dioxide is stored in water, plants, or in the ground, it can't contribute to global warming. The oceans have so far absorbed about 90 percent of the heat created by greenhouse gases.

But our oceans are struggling. Polluting chemicals and waste pour into the oceans every day. Runoff from large farms and ranches, liquid waste from factories, and oil spills from pipelines and ships poison the water, killing the animals and plants that make it their home. Overfishing drives many types of fish into decline, and sharks, dolphins, and whales get tangled in giant commercial fishing lines and nets.

Huge amounts of trash, especially plastic, float in the ocean water. Sometimes all this trash makes giant trash islands. Two of these islands are located in the Pacific Ocean off the coasts of California and Japan. They're made up mostly of teeny pieces of ground-up plastic.

Our ocean biome needs us, and we can help! If we just reduce our use of plastic—plastic bags, plastic food containers, plastic water bottles—we can send the signal to companies: Not so much plastic, please and thank you. I'm going to choose sustainable options—metal water bottle? Yes, please! Thanks, I don't need a plastic bag to hold my one apple.

So maybe you do wind up with some plastic—okay, it's part of our world right now. See if you can recycle it. Does your grocery store recycle plastic bags? Save up your family's bags and return them! You can usually recycle plastic bottles and jugs in your recycling bin at home. Plastic recycling isn't ideal—lots of plastic isn't recyclable and some of what you put in your bin never actually gets a new life, but it's better than a whole-hog landfill dump. Every little bit of effort helps keep our oceans the clean, healthy biome we need them to be.

HOW YOU CAN HELP

Beaches are part of the ocean biome, too—and they also need help! Plastic, Styrofoam, tires, bottles, and diapers all get washed up on the sand where they pollute the beach environment. Next time you're at the beach, consider cleaning some of it up!

HOW TO HOLD A BEACH CLEANUP

First, get permission to hold a cleanup. Who is in charge of the beach you have in mind? You might need to call local government offices to ask.

Then, gather your volunteers. Put the call out among your friends, on social media, and through community channels, like newsletters. Let everyone know that you'll be holding a beach cleanup, and tell them where it will be and when.

Next, find your supplies. You'll need big garbage bags, hand sanitizer, rubber gloves, and a first aid kit. Are you bringing supplies for everyone? Make sure you have enough. Want everyone to bring their own supplies? Be sure to put that in your communications.

Make a plan to get the trash and recyclables off the beach. Who will carry the heavy bags? Are you taking the trash to a trash facility or to a dumpster? Make sure you have permission to throw the bags away! What about the recyclables? Identify a recycling container or facility that will take what you collect. Be sure you know how you're getting the trash and recyclables from the beach to the dumpster or facility. Have volunteer drivers with cars or trucks ready and waiting when you're done with the cleanup.

As you pick up trash, be on the lookout for broken glass or sharp pieces of metal that could cut you. Separate cans, bottles, and other recyclables and put them in labeled bags. Be sure to take breaks for water, snacks, and rest. If you see any truly hazardous materials—like spilled oil, containers with chemicals, or syringes—don't pick them up. Tell an adult in charge or a local official.

Then take time to enjoy the pristine beach that you helped clean up!

Yikes! I'm grateful I've never found things like diapers or plastic at the beach in the Overworld. In my world, I love to see turtles around the beach, and it's especially beautiful to watch them hatch. On Earth, they might not have to worry about zombies or other dangerous mobs, but there are still many threats that sea creatures face—and you can help them survive.

HOW TO MAKE SEAFOOD CAKES

For a crispy coating, this recipe uses store-bought, dried bread crumbs. You could also use panko bread crumbs, crushed cornflakes, cracker crumbs, or finely crushed pretzels.

Serves 4 to 6

INGREDIENTS

1 pound cooked skinless fish fillet or crab (leftover cooked fish works great for this)

1 1/2 cups dried bread crumbs

1/2 cup finely chopped scallions, onions, or shallots

2/3 cup mayonnaise

Grated zest and juice of 1/2 lemon

1 large egg

1 teaspoon kosher salt

1/2 teaspoon freshly ground black pepper

Canola oil, for frying

I like to eat fish, and I like to eat cakes. Are seafood cakes cod and salmon on top of a cake with icing and a candle? No? Well, cod and salmon are two of my favorite foods in the Overworld, so I'm curious to see what else we can do with them.

DIRECTIONS

1. In a large bowl, flake the fish with a fork. Add 1 cup of the bread crumbs, the scallions, mayonnaise, lemon zest, lemon juice, egg, salt, and pepper. Cover and refrigerate for at least 1 hour (and up to 2) to allow the bread crumbs to absorb the liquid.

2. Form the mixture into 8 patties. Spread the remaining 1/2 cup bread crumbs on a plate. Press both sides of the patties into the bread crumbs to coat fully and set aside while you heat the oil.

3. Pour 1 inch of oil into a large skillet and heat over medium heat. A trick for testing whether the oil is hot enough is to stick the end of a wooden spoon into it, touching the bottom of the pot. If lots of little bubbles form around the wood, the oil is ready! (This should be 350° to 365°F.)

4. Add 4 cakes to the oil and cook, turning once, until browned and crunchy, about 3 minutes on each side. Repeat with the remaining cakes.

VARIATIONS

Salmon and Corn Cakes: Use salmon for the fish. Replace the bread crumbs with 1 1/2 cups cornflake crumbs. Make the fish mixture as directed, adding 4 chopped scallions and 1 cup corn kernels and increasing the lemon zest and lemon juice to use one whole lemon. The rest is the same.

Caribbean Cod Cakes: Start by making a spice mix: 1 tablespoon paprika, 1 tablespoon kosher salt, 1 1/2 teaspoons onion powder, 1 1/2 teaspoons garlic powder, 1 teaspoon dried thyme, 1 teaspoon dried oregano, 1 teaspoon freshly ground black pepper, and 1/2 teaspoon cayenne pepper. Use cooked cod or other whitefish for the fish. Make the fish mixture as directed, adding 3 chopped scallions, 1/2 chopped green bell pepper, 1/2 chopped red bell pepper, and 2 tablespoons of the spice mix. The rest is the same.

I don't know about you, but skewers make me think of swords. One of the most important weapons you can make in Minecraft is a sword, so it must be pretty special for this food to be swordlike. But I don't recommend you have sword fights at the dinner table with your kabobs!

JERK SHRIMP KABOBS

Jerk is a style of cooking that comes from Jamaica, where pieces of meat, fish, fruit, or vegetables are rubbed with a spice paste and grilled over wood.

Serves 4 to 6

INGREDIENTS

3 tablespoons light brown sugar

2 tablespoons dried thyme

1 tablespoon kosher salt

2 teaspoons ground allspice

2 teaspoons freshly ground black pepper

1/2 teaspoon cayenne pepper

1/2 teaspoon ground nutmeg

1 1/2 pounds large peeled and deveined shrimp

6 scallions, cut into 3-inch lengths

1/2 medium onion, cut into chunks

6 cloves garlic, cut into big pieces

2-inch piece fresh ginger, peeled and roughly chopped

2 tablespoons apple cider vinegar or distilled white vinegar

Juice of 2 limes

2 tablespoons soy sauce

2 tablespoons canola oil

DIRECTIONS

1. In a small bowl, stir together the brown sugar, thyme, salt, allspice, black pepper, cayenne, and nutmeg. Measure out half of the dry rub mixture and spoon it into a blender.

2. Take the rest of the dry rub and rub it into the shrimp. Transfer the shrimp to a zipper storage bag or glass bowl and set aside.

3. To the blender with the rub, add the scallions, onion, garlic, ginger, and vinegar and process until it's a nearly smooth paste.

4. Add the dry rub to the shrimp, mix, cover, and marinate in the fridge. The shrimp should marinate for no longer than 1 hour or it can become mealy.

5. When ready to cook, preheat the broiler to high or preheat a grill.

6. Remove the shrimp from the marinade and thread onto eight 10-inch skewers (bamboo, metal, or sugar cane; see Tip). Broil on high in the oven or grill over direct heat, turning once, 4 to 6 minutes on each side.

VARIATION

Jerk Chicken Kabobs: Follow the recipe for Jerk Shrimp Kabobs, substituting 1 1/2 pounds boneless, skinless chicken thighs, cut into 1 1/2-inch chunks for the shrimp. Marinate the chicken for at least 2 and up to 8 hours, refrigerated. Broil on high in the oven or grill over direct heat, turning once, 8 to 10 minutes on each side.

TIP: Because bamboo skewers are dry and can burn, they need to be soaked in water for at least 1 hour before you expose them to heat or they'll go up in flames!

GARLICKY RATATOUILLE KABOBS

A super-easy way to prep garlic is to grate peeled cloves on a box grater or cheese grater.

Serves 4 to 6

INGREDIENTS

MOP SAUCE

1/3 cup olive oil

3 cloves garlic, grated

1 juicy medium tomato, finely chopped

1 teaspoon kosher salt

1/2 teaspoon freshly ground black pepper

2 teaspoons chopped fresh rosemary

SKEWERS

2 Japanese eggplants (or an Italian eggplant)

2 small zucchini

2 small yellow squash or yellow zucchini

1 red onion, peeled and cut into 8 large chunks

1 red bell pepper, stemmed and seeded, cut into large chunks

8 (10-inch-long) fresh rosemary stems (leaves removed), or skewers

Cooking spray

I know all about stews in Minecraft, but ratatouille is a kind of stew that's new to me. You make it by combining all sorts of vegetables, including ones I don't have on my own farm. I'm excited to try all these new flavors!

DIRECTIONS

1. **Make the mop sauce:** In a small heavy saucepan, heat the olive oil over medium heat. Add the garlic and cook and stir until it begins to smell garlicky, 2 to 3 minutes. Stir in the tomato, salt, pepper, and rosemary and cook and stir until the tomato breaks down, about 10 minutes. Mash it with a fork and stir. Set aside.

2. Preheat the broiler to high or preheat a grill.

3. **For the skewers:** Trim the ends of the eggplant, zucchini, and squash, and cut them crosswise into thick slices. Thread all of the vegetables onto the rosemary stems or skewers. (Pierce through the skin, not the flesh.) Brush with the garlicky tomato mop sauce.

4. Coat a baking sheet with cooking spray. Broil the skewers on high on the greased baking sheet, or grill over direct heat until beginning to brown, 7 to 10 minutes. Turn, brush with more mop sauce, and continue to cook until they are browned and the edges are beginning to char, another 7 to 8 minutes.

So it turns out one of the fruits people on Earth most associate with the beach and ocean is the coconut because it grows near the coast. The outside shell of it is pretty hard, so I'm wondering: Can you use one as a bowl? But in case that doesn't work, coconuts can also be used in a whole variety of recipes, including our next one.

COCONUT GREEN CURRY CHICKEN AND RICE

In this recipe, the chicken is given a soft, velvety texture by rubbing it with baking soda. This will tenderize the chicken, then just rinse the chicken, pat dry, and cook according to the recipe.

Serves 4

DIRECTIONS

1. Cut the chicken crosswise into thin strips and transfer to a bowl. Toss with the baking soda and set aside for at least 15 minutes (but not more than 30).

2. In a large shallow pot, heat the oil over medium-high heat. Add the green beans and cook and stir until they begin to soften, about 5 minutes. Remove and keep warm.

3. Add the chicken to the same pot and cook and stir until no longer pink, 4 to 5 minutes.

4. Return the green beans to the pot along with the coconut milk, curry paste, fish sauce, lime zest, lime juice, chiles, brown sugar, and ginger. Bring to a boil, then reduce the heat to a simmer and cook until the green beans are tender, another few minutes.

5. Stir in the basil and serve over cooked rice or rice noodles.

TIP: If you want to try this baking-soda trick on other chicken, just use 1 1/2 teaspoons baking soda for every 1 pound of boneless chicken (let it sit for at least 15 minutes but not more than 30 minutes).

INGREDIENTS

1 pound boneless, skinless chicken breast

1 1/2 teaspoons baking soda

2 tablespoons canola oil or coconut oil

8 ounces green beans, trimmed

1 cup canned full-fat coconut milk

1/2 cup Thai green curry paste

2 tablespoons Thai fish sauce

Grated zest and juice of 1 lime

2 fresh hot red chiles, thinly sliced (1/3 cup)

1 tablespoon light brown sugar

1 teaspoon grated fresh ginger

A good handful (about 1/2 cup) fresh basil leaves, roughly chopped or torn apart

Cooked rice or rice noodles, for serving

After a good meal at the beach, it's time for dessert. Yum! Dulce de leche is a recipe that uses milk and sugar, so I can run off to milk a cow and get some sugar cane. Some of the other ingredients are specific to Earth, like your bananas. Even though a lot of people don't think of them this way, I'm reading that bananas are actually a berry. I have to say, though, they look a little different from the sweet berries I can get in Minecraft. Whatever they look like, this recipe tastes wonderful!

BANANA DULCE DE LECHE BATIDO

A batido is basically a milkshake or a creamy smoothie, popular in Latin America. A common ingredient is oats or puffed wheat, which helps thicken the batido and makes it extra healthy. (It's like a cereal smoothie!)

Serves 2

INGREDIENTS

1 cup canned full-fat coconut milk

1 banana, chunked

2 tablespoons quick-cooking oats

2 tablespoons prepared dulce de leche

A few ice cubes

Cinnamon, for sprinkling

DIRECTIONS

In a high-powdered blender, combine the coconut milk, banana, oats, dulce de leche, and ice and blend until thick and smooth, about 30 seconds. Sprinkle with the cinnamon.

FORESTS

Picture yourself surrounded by giant trees. Some of them are thirty years old. Some are four hundred years old. The air is damp and foggy. Under your feet, moss squishes. You have to clamber over massive crashed-over tree trunks, with branches jutting up like sentinels. Stop and look up. The trees soar overhead, so high you're dizzy trying to spot the tops.

Forests are magical, oxygen-saturated places to walk and dream. They're containers for human imagination. Earth's writers and artists have imagined elves and dybbuks and unicorns and centaurs making their homes in the mysterious forest. And forests aren't just receptacles for our romantic art. They're much more than a collection of trees, too.

When I go out into forests around here I run into skeletons, zombies, and creepers. I'm glad that the creatures in your forest don't sound quite so dangerous.

I'm also glad that your spiders are a lot smaller! It's just too bad it takes a lot longer for you to tame your wolves. Luckily, you already have dogs so you can skip that step.

Covering about one-third of the Earth's surface, the forest biome is home and food for huge numbers of animals and insects. In temperate forests, which have distinct seasons, the trees lose their leaves each fall, creating leaf litter that covers the forest floor. Snakes, insects, and small rodents, like mice, live in and under the leaf litter. Meanwhile, depending on the continent, black and brown bears, wallabies, sugar gliders, foxes, macaques, or raccoons might roam above, hunting, eating, and making their nests and dens in holes, hollow logs, and small caves. Tree roots, extending down into the earth, hang on to the soil and keep it from eroding.

Forests release giant amounts of oxygen into the atmosphere and take in and store the carbon dioxide that is causing climate change. When they take in CO_2, they also take in pollutants in the air, like giant air-scrubbers. The trees grow, and as they do, they suck in carbon dioxide from the atmosphere and store it. The smaller plants in the forest store carbon dioxide, too, and so does the ground. The CO_2 is safely tucked away, rather than swimming around in our atmosphere, causing climate chaos like an unruly houseguest.

But when people cut down forests, for timber or to clear space, all that carbon dioxide is released. The same thing happens when people burn forests. In fact, in the last 150 years or so, almost one-third of all carbon dioxide emissions have come from deforestation. Plus, forests release cool, moist air all around them. When they're gone—*boom*—the air gets hotter and drier, which also means things are hotter and drier for people and animals.

Help! What can humans do to help Earth's forests? Rewilding is one answer, and it's pretty simple—allow forests to regrow on their own. Without human interference, saplings will regrow and the deforested area will eventually return to the way it was. To help support our forest biome, look for products from companies that support sustainable forests. Keep an eye out for recycled paper and wood-fiber products. That way, our forests can keep doing their job on our planet.

HOW YOU CAN HELP

You probably can't grow a forest in your backyard, and you definitely can't grow one on your balcony or deck, but you can grow a smaller version—a garden!

PLANT A GARDEN

YOU WILL NEED:

Topsoil and compost, either bagged or loose

Spade and trowel

Seeds and seedlings

Watering can or garden hose

Clothes you can get dirty in

A plot of ground or several large flowerpots (the kind with holes in the bottom)

Let's plant!

■ Choose either a sunny corner of a deck, porch, or balcony for pots or a sunny, flat piece of ground.

■ If your garden is on a plot of ground, use your spade to dig up any grass or other plants already in the spot.

■ Then mix up some topsoil and compost into a nice, yummy, good-smelling pile. Shovel it into your pots, if you're using them, or spread it on your garden plot and blend it with the soil using your spade.

■ Time to get those seeds in the ground! Read the directions on the seed packets and follow them carefully. Dig holes to the directed depth and space them apart according to the instructions.

■ After you cover the seeds with dirt, give them a good watering. Try to gently sprinkle the water so you don't blast away all your topsoil!

■ Then, keep an eye on your babies. You might need a small fence around your garden plot if rabbits and other small critters start eating your shoots.

■ Once your veggies are ready to harvest—pick and eat! You're a gardener now!

In Minecraft, everyone does at least a little bit of planting. It's an amazing way to get your hands on a steady source of tasty food without having to leave your home!

Remember that compost we made in the Plains chapter? Growing plants is what it's all about.

HOW TO MAKE
APPLESAUCE

Applesauce is one of the most fun things to make as a group. One person can peel, one can remove the stem and seeds, another can cut the apples into chunks, and you can all take turns stirring and smashing.

Makes 1 quart

INGREDIENTS

Juice of ½ lemon

1 cup water

1 cinnamon stick (optional), broken in half (this releases flavor)

Pinch of salt

3 pounds soft, sweet apples, such as Golden Delicious, McIntosh, Rome, Fuji, Mutsu, or Cortland—or a mixture

Sugar, honey, or maple syrup

I love apples! They're one of my favorite things to eat when I need to get my health back up. I gather them from oak and dark oak leaves here in Minecraft, but I guess on Earth they grow on apple trees. Weird!

Earth has thousands of kinds of cultivated apples. Minecraft has only two, but my variant is a doozy: golden apples can help more with my health and can turn zombie villagers back into villagers. This here might not be a golden apple, but when you mash apples to make applesauce, you'll get a golden color.

DIRECTIONS

1. In a large deep pot over medium-high heat, stir together the lemon juice, water, cinnamon (if using), and salt.

2. Peel, core, and chunk the apples and add them to the pot as you work. Stir to coat the apples with the liquid.

3. Bring the pot to a boil. Stir, reduce the heat to a simmer, and cook slowly, stirring occasionally, until the apples are soft and broken down, about 40 minutes. If you've used crisp apples, you may want to mash them.

4. Remove the cinnamon stick. Sweeten the apples if you like, then smash with a potato masher or blend with a stick blender.

VARIATION

Rosy Applesauce: Follow the recipe for Basic Applesauce, adding 1 pint red berries (raspberries, strawberries, cranberries) with the apples. Makes 5 cups.

APPLESAUCE SNACKING CAKE

If you've made your own applesauce, this is a super-easy cake to make—or even easier with store-bought applesauce. You can experiment with the dried fruit and spices, if you like. There are some combos to try at the end of this recipe.

Serves 9

INGREDIENTS

Cooking spray
½ cup canola oil
½ cup packed light brown sugar
½ cup granulated sugar
1 large egg
1⅓ cups applesauce, store-bought or homemade (see page 40)
1 teaspoon vanilla extract
Grated zest of 1 lemon
2¼ cups all-purpose flour
1 teaspoon baking powder
1 teaspoon baking soda
1 teaspoon ground cinnamon
½ teaspoon ground cloves
½ teaspoon ground nutmeg
½ teaspoon kosher salt
½ cup raisins
Powdered sugar, for dusting

This golden apple cake might not help turn a zombie village back into a regular village, but it tastes so good I can't hold it against it! I would love to eat this when I'm mining.

DIRECTIONS

1. Preheat the oven to 350°F. Coat a 9-inch square baking pan with cooking spray.

2. In a large bowl, beat together the canola oil, brown sugar, and granulated sugar. Add the egg, applesauce, vanilla, and lemon zest one at a time, mixing well after each addition.

3. In a separate bowl, stir together the flour, baking powder, baking soda, all the spices, and the salt. Now add the dry ingredients to the applesauce mixture, stirring until all of the flour is mixed in. Stir in the raisins.

4. Scrape the batter into the prepared pan and bake until the top springs back when lightly touched, 20 to 25 minutes.

5. Serve warm or cool and dust with a bit of powdered sugar.

VARIATIONS

Omit the lemon zest and use the grated zest of 1 orange in its place. Substitute dried cranberries for the raisins.

Add chopped pears and walnuts. Add 1 teaspoon ground cardamom or ginger to the cinnamon. Omit the cloves and nutmeg.

Omit the lemon zest. Add 1 teaspoon maple extract. Stir in ½ cup chopped dates.

When I'm cooking, it's usually with an eye for speed. After all, if a zombie is trying to get into the kitchen, you want your cooked porkchops fast! Since (hopefully) that's not a concern for you, try taking your time on this one—it'll be worth the wait!

DIRECTIONS

1. Preheat the oven to 350°F.

2. Begin by preparing the meat. If the recipe calls for marinating the meat before cooking, now is the time to remove it from the marinade and pat it dry.

3. In a heavy pot or Dutch oven with a lid, heat the oil over medium-high heat and brown the meat very well on all sides. The darker it gets, the richer the flavor, so take your time! Remove the meat and set aside.

4. In the same pot, cook and stir any vegetables you're using until browned.

5. Add liquid to the pan and stir with a wooden spoon, scraping up any browned bits stuck to the pot. This is called deglazing. Turn the heat down to simmer.

6. Add the meat back to the pot along with any juices collected on the plate, cover, and cook low and slow until the meat is tender.

HOW TO BRAISE OR STEW

Braising means cooking a tough piece of meat or poultry at a lower temperature for a long time in some liquid. Cooking low and slow softens the meat until it falls apart with a fork and makes the whole kitchen smell delicious. Stewing is basically just another word for braising. Any leftover meat can be shredded and used for sandwiches.

INGREDIENTS

Chicken or beef, size and cut of your choosing

Vegetable oil

Vegetables, such as onions, carrots, and potatoes

Water

Sometimes baby zombies ride around on chickens, but that's not what I use them for. Chickens are special because they not only can supply meat, but they can also give us eggs and feathers. And on Earth, you can turn them into lots of recipes, including this one!

CHICKEN CACCIATORE

Say "Catch-a-TORE-y." It means "hunter style" in Italian. You can serve the chicken with crusty bread to mop up all the sauce or do as they do in Italy: serve the sauce on pasta and the chicken alongside.

Serves 4

INGREDIENTS

3 tablespoons olive oil

3 pounds bone-in chicken pieces

1 medium onion, chopped

3 nice fat cloves garlic, sliced

1 (15-ounce) can chicken broth

1 (28-ounce) can whole peeled tomatoes, undrained

1 bay leaf

1 sprig fresh rosemary

1 teaspoon kosher salt

Red pepper flakes (optional)

DIRECTIONS

1. In a Dutch oven or shallow heavy pot, heat the olive oil over medium-high heat. Add the chicken pieces a few at a time and cook until well browned on both sides. Remove to a plate while you cook the rest.

2. Add the onion and garlic to the pan and cook and stir until softened and beginning to brown, about 5 minutes.

3. Reduce the heat to low and pour in the broth, deglazing the pot by scraping up the browned bits with a wooden spoon. They'll dissolve and add a lot of flavor to the dish.

4. One by one, crush the canned tomatoes with your hands as you add them to the pan, but discard the tough little stem end with the stringy bits attached.

Pour in the juices from the tomato can and add the bay leaf, rosemary, salt, and pepper flakes to taste (if using).

5. Bring to a simmer. Add the chicken and any juice that has accumulated on the plate. Cover and simmer until the chicken is fork tender, about 40 minutes.

CUBAN PORK
(LECHON ASADO)

Leftover shredded Cuban pork warmed with a little barbecue sauce makes the BEST pulled pork!

Serves 8 (with leftovers)

INGREDIENTS

5 to 6 pounds boneless pork shoulder

8 nice fat cloves garlic

2 teaspoons dried oregano

2 teaspoons ground cumin

2 tablespoons kosher salt

2 teaspoons freshly ground black pepper

4 tablespoons olive oil

Juice of 3 lemons

Juice of 1 orange

3 tablespoons red wine vinegar

I know about eating a porkchop, but this kind of pork is all new to me, and it seems a lot fancier. In this recipe you take a boneless pork shoulder and add all sorts of spices and even some fruit. And this meal is set to have leftovers, so it will keep your hunger bar full for a while.

DIRECTIONS

1. With a sharp knife, poke deep holes all over the meat, on both sides.

2. In a blender or with a mortar and pestle, blend the garlic, oregano, cumin, salt, pepper, and 2 tablespoons of the olive oil to a paste.

3. Push the garlic paste into all the holes in the meat and place the meat in a zipper storage bag. Pour in the lemon juice, orange juice, and vinegar. Seal and refrigerate overnight or for up to 2 days.

4. Remove the meat from the marinade and pat dry. (Save the marinade!)

5. Preheat the oven to 350°F.

6. In a heavy ovenproof pot with a lid or a Dutch oven, heat the remaining 2 tablespoons oil over medium-high heat. Add the meat and brown well on all sides.

7. Add the reserved marinade, cover, and transfer to the oven to bake until fork tender, about 4 hours. Check once an hour and if the liquid evaporates, add 1 cup water or broth.

8. Either cut into thick slices or pull apart with two forks into chunks.

Okay, so these aren't actual mushrooms. But you can design these cupcakes to look like mushrooms! I like to use my world's cocoa pods to make cookies, and this recipe shows how cocoa can be used to make these cupcakes! In addition to that, this recipe calls for milk, just like the milk that helped me after I ate all those poisonous potatoes. . . .

They might not be as big as huge mushrooms, but they will still give you plenty to eat. And, like mushrooms, these cupcake mushrooms are going to be someplace without a lot of sunlight—in our stomachs!

DIRECTIONS

1. **Make the cupcakes:** Preheat the oven to 350°F. Line 9 cups of a standard muffin tin and 9 cups of a mini muffin tin with paper liners. Coat the liners with cooking spray.

2. In a bowl, whisk together the condensed milk, canola oil, vanilla, vinegar, and milk.

3. In another bowl, sift together the flour, cornstarch, cocoa, baking powder, baking soda, and salt. Now gently combine the milk mixture with the flour mixture. Do not overmix.

4. Fill the prepared muffin tin cups three-quarters full of batter (we want it to overflow, to create the mushroom cap).

5. Bake until a toothpick inserted in the center comes out with no batter sticking to it, 15 minutes for minis and another 3 to 4 minutes for the large.

RECIPE CONTINUES

BLACK FOREST "MUSHROOM" CAKES

The Black Forest is in Germany, where mushrooms grow wild and Black Forest cake hails from. These little cakes might look like mushrooms, but they taste like delicious, chocolaty Black Forest cake.

Makes 9 cupcakes

INGREDIENTS

CUPCAKES

Cooking spray

1 (14-ounce) can sweetened condensed milk

½ cup canola oil

1 teaspoon vanilla extract

1 teaspoon vinegar, any kind

½ cup milk

1¼ cups unbleached all-purpose flour

¼ cup cornstarch

½ cup unsweetened cocoa powder

1 teaspoon baking powder

½ teaspoon baking soda

¼ teaspoon salt

INGREDIENTS CONTINUE

INGREDIENTS (CONT.)

WHITE CHOCOLATE GANACHE

1/2 cup white chocolate chips,
  plus 1/3 cup for decorating
3 tablespoons heavy cream
Red gel or paste food coloring

CHOCOLATE GANACHE

1 cup semisweet chocolate chips
3/4 cup heavy cream

ASSEMBLY

8 ounces cherry preserves
1/3 cup white chocolate chips
Dark green sprinkles or chopped
  pistachios

6. Cool completely in the pan.

7. **Make the white chocolate ganache:** In a small microwave-safe bowl, mix the white chocolate chips and cream and microwave in 15-second increments, stirring well after each until melted. Let the mixture cool at room temperature to spreading consistency, about 1 hour—or in the fridge, about 20 minutes.

8. **Make the chocolate ganache:** In a small microwave-safe bowl, mix the chocolate chips and cream and microwave in 15-second increments, stirring well after each until melted. Let the mixture cool at room temperature to spreading consistency, about 1 hour—or in the fridge, about 20 minutes.

9. **To assemble:** With a small spoon, scoop out a tablespoon full of cake from the top of each large cupcake and reserve the cake crumbs. (The diameter of the hole should be no more than 1 1/2 inches.)

10. Fill the hole with cherry preserves almost to the top. Finish filling all of the large cupcakes. Crumble the cake crumbs to look like dirt. Frost the cupcakes with the chocolate ganache and sprinkle with the cake crumbs, avoiding the center hole.

11. Color the white chocolate ganache with the red food coloring. Frost the tops of the mini cupcakes and decorate with the white chocolate chips, pointed end down, flat-side up. Remove the mini cupcakes from their paper casings and place on top of the larger cupcakes, into the indentation left by the excavation.

12. Sprinkle green sprinkles around the base of the mushrooms to look like moss.

Mushrooms like to grow in dark places, like in a forest. I can take mushrooms to make mushroom stew, rabbit stew, and suspicious stew. Of course some mushrooms I can't eat—they're too giant! I'm learning on Earth it's the same way. Only some mushrooms are for eating because some other kinds can make people sick, so you don't just eat any mushroom you find.

MUSHROOM BARLEY SOUP

You can use any kind of mushrooms in this recipe, but I like morels and porcini best. This soup is even better the next day!

Serves 6 (with leftovers)

DIRECTIONS

1. In a small heatproof bowl, pour just enough boiling water over the dried mushrooms to cover them. Set aside until the mushrooms are softened and the water is cool, about 45 minutes.

2. Scoop the mushrooms from the soaking water and chop. Line a small sieve with a paper towel and strain the soaking liquid through it into a small bowl.

3. In a large heavy pot, heat the oil over medium-high heat until you see it shimmer. Add the onion, celery, carrots, parsnips, fresh mushrooms, and thyme and cook and stir until they begin to soften and brown, 5 to 8 minutes.

4. Add the mushrooms, soaking liquid, broth, and barley and season with salt and pepper. Bring to a simmer and cook, stirring occasionally, until the barley has cooked and thickened the broth, about 45 minutes.

INGREDIENTS

Boiling water

4 dried mushrooms

1 tablespoon canola oil

1 medium onion, chopped

2 stalks celery, chunked

2 medium carrots, peeled and chunked

2 parsnips, turnips, rutabagas, or potatoes, peeled and chunked

1 pound fresh cremini, portobello, or white mushrooms, trimmed and sliced

1 teaspoon dried thyme or 3 sprigs fresh

3 quarts vegetable or beef broth

1 cup pearl barley

Kosher salt and freshly ground black pepper

RIVERS

A river can be a slow, meandering stream, flat and glassy between grassy banks. Or it can be a wild, white-frothed torrent pounding between rock faces, with huge rocks tumbling along its bottom like pebbles. Or how about a golden-watered creek flowing at the bottom of a forest slope, with limestone rocks and blackberry brambles lining its edges?

I love taking a nice boat cruise down a river, as long as I can keep those pesky drowned away. Which shouldn't be a problem for you. Just make sure you've packed your life vest, since there's no potions of Water Breathing over there!

I hear some Earth rivers, like the Nile, go on for thousands of miles! You'd need a lot of snacks to row all that way.

Minecraft water doesn't exactly differentiate between salty and fresh. But on Earth that determines what ecosystems a body of water has. I guess that's why you folks don't have river squids, huh?

Rivers might look all kinds of ways, but they always have fresh water. They originate at headwaters, like a lake, a glacier, or a spring. Then they cut a channel through the land, with water moving in one direction (that's the current of the river). Rivers always end at another body of water, like an ocean or another river. This is called the mouth of the river.

Frogs, herons, trout, carp, egrets, crayfish, salamanders, crocodiles, water skippers, ducks, platypuses, turtles, porpoises, otters—this is only a partial list of all the animals and insects that live in and around rivers. Freshwater clams are food for crayfish, which in turn are food for water snakes, which are then eaten by hawks, which soar overhead or perch on overhanging branches. Frogs eat water skaters, then herons snack on frogs. In this incredibly rich biome, cattails, lily pads, algae, and mosses drink up the watery environment they love.

Picture a really dirty sink. Hair, soap scum, nail clippings. The water swishes around the porcelain and all that gunk goes into the drain. This somewhat gross image is a pretty accurate representation of what happens to rivers. These vital waterways are basically the drain for the landscape. All the gunk in the surrounding land—pesticides, chemicals, agricultural runoff like manure, and factory runoff—drains or is washed by stormwater into nearby rivers, leaving them polluted. The way to keep our rivers clean is to keep our landscape clean! Pesticides on farms—pesticides in the river. Factory chemical runoff on land—straight into the river.

So take your hazardous household materials—like old paint or motor oil—to a hazardous materials recycling center. Don't dump it down drains or in sewers. Does your family use a septic system? Have it checked every year! You don't want to be leaking what you flush down the toilet into a nearby creek (eww!). And that lawn out front? See if you and your family can live with a few dandelions and weeds. The pesticide and herbicide spray gets washed away by rainwater, down into the sewers—and you guessed it—into the nearest river biome. And don't forget creeks and streams. These smaller waterways feed into larger rivers. The pollutants in one drain into the waters of the other. Our river biome is full of sprawling watery connections—and needs us to help keep it healthy and clean.

HOW YOU CAN HELP

Creeks and rivers often run right through our cities and neighborhoods. The animals in these biomes need protection from urban sprawl. Make a safe space for mammals and insects in your own backyard.

CREATE A WILDLIFE HABITAT

You don't need acres and acres of space to make a refuge for animals. A small yard, a deck, or a balcony can all become a safe place for small mammals and birds.

Just like you, animals need high-quality nutrition. Delicious natural food sources will attract them—kind of like a doughnut shop might attract you. Planting colorful flowers in your yard or in pots on your deck will attract butterflies. Sunflowers entice the birds. But the most important plants to attract animals are native ones. Some quick research can give you a list of native plants for your area. Then get some seedlings or seeds and get growing!

Next, water! Install a birdbath, a small pool, or even just a few shallow pans of water beside your plant pots. Put a few rocks in, too. That way, if insects land in the water by accident, they can swim over to a rock, climb on, and fly away. Just be sure to empty and change the water every couple of days in the summer—otherwise, you'll be creating a lovely mosquito nursery.

Then, if you've got space, think bushes, shrubs, and tall grasses. Wildlife feels safer when they have places to hide. If you already have bushes in your backyard, put your food and water sources near them. If you don't, or if you're on a deck or a balcony, think of getting a couple shrubs in pots to give the birds and animals some cover.

For the birds, help them find a safe place to nest away from cats and other predators. Hang bird nest boxes around your habitat, or on the branches of your potted shrubs.

You can also add dead logs and branches and piles of leaves and sticks. These offer shelter and good hiding places for small rodents and other animals. Beetles and other insects love dead logs.

Then, grab your binoculars and your wildlife-recording notebook and wait. The animals will be there before you know it!

In Minecraft I might be able to tame mobs like parrots or ocelots, but these Earth animals are going to stay wild. I don't recommend you try to pet them. But they'll love the gifts you give them just as much!

HOW TO COOK RICE

Rice is one of the simplest things to cook, especially if you follow these directions. Most important, ALWAYS rinse your rice and NEVER stir it while cooking or you'll end up with gummy, sticky rice. Although if that happens, just make rice porridge (see page 58)!

Serves 4

INGREDIENTS

1 cup long-grain or short-grain white rice

2 cups water, broth, or unsweetened coconut water

½ teaspoon salt

In some parts of the world, rice is grown in terraces carved from mountainsides. Some of them are thousands of years old! The flat surfaces going down the hills are beautiful . . . hey, they kind of look Minecrafty, don't they?

DIRECTIONS

1. Place the rice in a fine-mesh sieve and rinse it with cold water until the water runs clear.

2. Add the rice to a medium saucepan along with the water and salt. Bring it to a boil over high heat. Reduce the heat to medium and cook uncovered until you see the grains of rice poking up above the water, about 10 minutes. Now cover the saucepan and cook for another 5 minutes.

3. Turn the heat off and leave the rice for 10 minutes to allow it to steam.

RICE PORRIDGE, SWEET OR SAVORY

Rice porridge is a common food across Asia. In China it's called congee and in Korea it's called juk. No matter the name, rice porridge is just the thing when you have an upset tummy.

Serves 2 or 3

Rice porridge is good for an upset tummy, huh? Does that mean it would be good to add to a potion of Healing, to amplify the effect like glowstone dust does? Well, even if it doesn't do that, this sounds like a simple, clean, yummy meal to help someone feel better.

SAVORY PORRIDGE

INGREDIENTS

1 cup Basic Cooked Rice (page 56)

2 cups chicken or vegetable broth

TOPPINGS

Cooked egg

Warmed stewed tomatoes

Grated cheese

Chopped cooked ham or bacon

Drizzle of toasted sesame oil

Anything else that sounds good to you

DIRECTIONS

In a medium saucepan, stir together the cooked rice and broth and bring to a boil over high heat. Reduce the heat to medium and cook, stirring constantly, until the porridge thickens and the rice falls apart, about 45 minutes. Serve warm with the toppings of your choice.

SWEET PORRIDGE

INGREDIENTS

1 cup Basic Cooked Rice (page 56) or any leftover rice

2 cups any sort of milk (coconut milk is really good!)

Maple syrup, honey, or whatever sweetener you like

TOPPINGS

Chopped apple or pear

Dried fruit

Coconut flakes

Nuts

A sprinkling of cinnamon, nutmeg, or cardamom

Anything else that sounds good to you

DIRECTIONS

In a medium saucepan, stir together the cooked rice and milk and bring to a boil over high heat. Reduce the heat to medium and cook, stirring constantly, until the porridge thickens and the rice falls apart, about 30 minutes. Stir in sweetener to taste. Serve warm with whatever toppings you want.

This rice is going to be pink, but it would not be dyed the way I'm used to making things pink! There are a few ways I can get pink dye. One is from collecting flowers like a peony or pink tulip. I can also craft pretty pink dye from white and red dye. I don't recommend you put tulips in your rice, but I hope you enjoy the pink color!

DIRECTIONS

1. Place the rice in a fine-mesh sieve and rinse it with cold water until the water runs clear.

2. In a medium saucepan, heat the oil over medium heat. Add the rice and cook, stirring, until it starts to turn white, about 3 minutes. Add the garlic and cook for another minute.

3. Add the broth, salt, tomato sauce, and cumin and bring to a boil over high heat.

4. Reduce the heat to medium and cook uncovered until you see the grains of rice poking up above the water, about 10 minutes. Now cover the saucepan and cook another 5 minutes.

5. Turn the heat off and leave the rice for 10 minutes to allow it to steam.

SPANISH PINK RICE

If you've ever had Spanish—or Mexican—rice at a restaurant, you know that it has a slightly drier, chewier texture. This comes from quickly frying the rice in a little bit of oil before adding the liquid. You could add some shredded cooked chicken and peas with the broth and turn this into a full meal.

Serves 4

INGREDIENTS

1 cup long-grain rice
2 tablespoons vegetable oil
1 nice fat clove garlic, grated
1¹⁄₂ cups chicken or vegetable broth
¹⁄₂ teaspoon salt
¹⁄₂ cup tomato sauce
¹⁄₄ teaspoon ground cumin

Where I'm from, things are naturally cubes. On Earth that isn't the case, but it's a neat trick that you can turn some things square-shaped by putting them in ice cube trays. Since this recipe is from Japan, I've been learning how to use chopsticks, and I can't wait to try them on this dish!

DIRECTIONS

1. Follow the directions in Basic Cooked Rice (page 56) to cook the rice, using the rice, water, and salt amounts listed here.

2. While the rice is cooking, in a small saucepan heat the vinegar and sugar, stirring until the sugar is dissolved. You can also mix them in a small bowl and microwave for a minute.

3. As soon as the rice finishes steaming, spread it out on a baking sheet and drizzle evenly with the vinegar mixture. Use a silicone spatula to gently but quickly turn the rice over and move it around until the vinegar is absorbed. It will become sticky, which is what you want. Let it cool to room temperature.

4. Spray an ice cube tray with cooking spray or rub with vegetable oil. Place a piece of topping (about 1 teaspoon) in the bottom of each prepared ice cube compartment. Top with the sushi rice and press down to pack tightly. Once the whole tray is filled, turn it over onto a plate and tap the tray to remove the blocks. Serve immediately.

ICE CUBE TRAY SUSHI BLOCKS

If you don't have ice cube trays, you can make these in mini muffin pans or just pile the rice into small bowls and let everybody choose their own toppings.

Serves 4 to 6

INGREDIENTS

1 cup short-grain rice

1½ cups water

½ teaspoon salt

2 tablespoons unseasoned rice vinegar

2 teaspoons sugar

Cooking spray or vegetable oil, for the ice cube tray

TOPPINGS

Thin slices of raw or smoked salmon

Cucumber

Avocado

Peanuts

Mango

Leftover cooked eggs

Drained canned tuna

Mayonnaise

Chopped scallions

CREAMY SQUASH AND PARMESAN RISOTTO

Now that you've learned how to cook rice, we're throwing you a curveball with risotto. It's totally different—creamy instead of fluffy, and you eat it in a bowl like pasta. Play around and replace the squash with any other kind of cooked vegetable that sounds good to you; just follow the same basic instructions.

Serves 4

INGREDIENTS

1 cup mashed cooked winter squash (or canned pumpkin)

4 cups chicken or vegetable broth

4 tablespoons butter

1 medium onion, chopped

1 cup short-grain rice, such as Arborio or Carnaroli rice

Salt and freshly ground black pepper

A pinch of grated nutmeg

3/4 cup grated parmesan cheese

A few roasted pumpkin seeds or walnuts (optional), for garnish

I'm learning that squash is from the same family as pumpkins. That helps me understand them better because I know all about pumpkins. I can trade them, I can carve them, and I can use them to make a snow golem. I can also wear one on my head and I think it looks pretty scary, but it's hard to see when I have it on. It also makes it hard to eat. I'm gonna take it off to enjoy this dish.

DIRECTIONS

1. In a saucepan, stir together the squash and broth and heat over low heat. Keep warm.

2. In a heavy-bottomed saucepan or Dutch oven, melt 2 tablespoons of the butter over medium heat. Add the onion and rice and cook and stir until the onions start to soften and the rice becomes white/opaque, about 5 minutes.

3. Add 1/2 cup of the warm broth mixture and stir constantly until the liquid is absorbed. Add the salt, pepper, and nutmeg. Turn the heat down a bit so it doesn't sputter too much. Continue to ladle more liquid in, about 1/2 cup at a time, stirring until the liquid is absorbed. When all the liquid has been used, the risotto should be the consistency of oatmeal—not dry, not too soupy.

4. Turn the heat off and stir in the remaining 2 tablespoons butter and the parmesan.

5. Serve immediately. If desired, garnish with pumpkin seeds.

HOW TO
BOIL AN EGG

The main thing to remember is that the fresher an egg is, the stronger the shell clings to it, making it nearly impossible to peel easily. An egg that is a week or two old is best for boiling. Following are the steps to boil a large egg.

The first time I ever saw someone eating an egg by itself, it blew my mind! I had always baked them into cakes or pies. Naturally I had to try it for myself. I went back to Minecraft, found an egg, cracked the shell . . . and it spawned a chicken.

That isn't how it works on Earth, I know, but my point is that cracking a raw egg gets messy. Boil 'em first!

DIRECTIONS

1. Place your egg(s) in a saucepan just large enough to hold it/them. Cover with cold water.

2. Bring the egg(s) to a full, lively boil over high heat.

3. Remove the pan from the heat and cover. Let the egg(s) sit in the hot water until done the way you like (see Egg Doneness, at right).

4. Remove from the pan and run under very cold water until the egg(s) is/are cool enough to handle. Tap it/them all over and peel.

EGG DONENESS

Runny egg: Let them sit for 2 to 3 minutes.

Jammy egg: Let them sit for 4 to 5 minutes.

Hard-cooked (but not dry) egg: Let them sit for 6 to 8 minutes.

Hard-boiled egg: Let them sit for 10 minutes.

If you want to knock a mob back but not actually hurt it, you can throw an egg at it. But if you throw an egg at a mob that isn't bothering you, it might start bothering you. And if you throw eggs around on Earth, you just make a mess. So I don't recommend you throw eggs around!

DIRECTIONS

1. In a heatproof container just large enough to hold the eggs, stir together the boiling water and sugar until the sugar dissolves. Stir in the soy sauce and vinegar.

2. Peel the eggs and add them to the soy mixture. If they pop up above the liquid, place a small saucer or plate on top to make sure they're submerged. Cover and refrigerate for at least 1 hour and up to 2 days.

SOY SAUCE EGGS

If you've made some rice porridge (see page 58), one of these eggs is super tasty on top. Or in ramen noodles (an easy way to jazz up the packaged ones!), or as a sweet and savory snack on its own. You can continue to use the liquid over and over with new batches of eggs.

Serves 4

INGREDIENTS

½ cup boiling water

2 teaspoons sugar or honey

½ cup soy sauce

1 tablespoon cider vinegar

4 large eggs, freshly hard-boiled (see opposite page)

DEVILED EGGS

Never mind their name, these eggs are heavenly! To "devil" something just means to mix it with mustard or something else spicy. Keep them refrigerated until just before you eat them.

Makes 8 deviled eggs

INGREDIENTS

4 large eggs, hard-boiled (see page 64)

2 tablespoons mayonnaise

1 teaspoon prepared mustard

1 teaspoon pickle juice, from sweet or sour pickles

Paprika, for sprinkling

Finely chopped pickles (optional), for garnish

Here's another egg recipe. Every now and then I see a fox carrying an egg around. I could ask the fox to share with me, but honestly I don't think foxes are going to like the same egg recipes that humans do.

DIRECTIONS

1. After boiling and cooling the eggs, refrigerate for at least 2 hours or overnight. This firms up the egg white so they don't collapse when you fill them.

2. Peel the eggs and slice in half lengthwise. Place the halves face up on a serving plate.

3. Pop out the yolks into a small bowl and mash with a fork until smooth. Stir in the mayonnaise, mustard, and pickle juice.

4. Scrape the mixture into a small zipper storage bag, snip off a corner, and squeeze it into the egg halves, or just use a teaspoon to fill them. Sprinkle the eggs with some paprika and top with a bit of chopped pickle, if you like. Serve immediately or cover and refrigerate for up to a day.

If I get four blocks of packed mud, I can make myself some mud bricks. This is a very different kind of mud, though! I don't know about building with these, but that's okay. I bet they taste a lot better.

MISSISSIPPI MUD BLOCKS

These chocolaty, fudgy, nutty bars share their name with other chocolate desserts from Mississippi. Why? Because some folks think the chocolate looks like the mud from the banks of the Mississippi River. That would make for some mighty tasty bricks!

Makes 24 bars

INGREDIENTS

Cooking spray and flour for the baking pan

2 cups semisweet chocolate chips

2 sticks (8 ounces) butter

1¼ cups sugar

1 teaspoon vanilla extract

½ teaspoon salt

4 large eggs

1½ cups all-purpose flour

TOPPING

1 cup heavy cream

1 cup semisweet chocolate chips

1 cup chopped pecans, peanuts, or walnuts, toasted

A sprinkle of flaky salt (optional)

DIRECTIONS

1. Spray a 9 × 13-inch baking pan with cooking spray and lightly coat with flour.

2. In a large saucepan, combine the chocolate chips and butter and stir constantly over low heat until melted and smooth. (Alternatively, place the chocolate and butter in a microwave-safe bowl and microwave in 15-second increments, stirring well after each, until melted and smooth.)

3. Remove from the heat and, with a wire whisk, stir in the sugar, vanilla, and salt. Then beat in the eggs one at a time, whisking well after each egg. Switch to a silicone spatula and stir in the flour.

4. Spread the batter evenly in the prepared baking pan and bake until the top is no longer jiggly, 15 to 20 minutes. Remove from the oven and let it cool in the pan while you prepare the topping.

5. **Make the topping:** In a small saucepan, heat the cream over medium heat until bubbles start to appear around the edges. Remove from the heat and stir in the chocolate chips. Cover the pan and let it sit for a few minutes to let the chocolate melt. Uncover and stir together until smooth.

6. Sprinkle the nuts evenly over the top of the bars and pour the chocolate evenly over that.

7. Cover loosely and let the bars cool completely before you cut them. You can even refrigerate them overnight to make them super easy to cut.

8. If you like, sprinkle a tiny bit of flaky salt on top just before you serve.

MOUNTAINS

Soaring tens of thousands of feet into the atmo-sphere, the alpine biomes on our planet are icy, cold, and rocky. Venture up a mountain and the trees go from decid-uous, to evergreen, to nonexistent—large trees can't handle the low temperatures high up in the mountain biome. Keep going beyond the tree line, and, at some point past ten thousand feet, you'll be tramping around in snow, even in July.

Even though mountains are tough places to live, some plants and animals still call the alpine ranges of the world home. Lichen and mosses huddle close to the rocks. They don't need much air or dirt to live. Some lichen can go through photosynthesis at any temperature above 32°F. Other low-growing cushion plants huddle just below the wind roaring above them, sending down long taproots into the soil so they don't get whirled off the ridge. Dry, woody grasses and shrubs can handle snow and freezing temperatures without dying.

Wow! I'd love to take an elytra flight off one of these....

I hear that it takes millions of years of tectonic forces to create mountains. I also hear that some mountains were made with cooled lava. I've seen cobblestone created the same way!

Earth's mountain animals are good at living in this extreme biome, too. Many hibernate in snowy dens and sleep their way through the coldest months. Chinchillas, who make their home in the Andes mountains, have thick, soft fur to protect them from the snow and cold. Mountain goats easily scramble over rocks with their special grippy hooves. Burrow under the snow and you'll find tiny rodents like red-backed voles and deer mice. These smallest mountain inhabitants gather all the food they need during the summer, then dig deep tunnels and let the falling snow insulate them, keeping them warm so that they can stay active even during the harshest alpine winter.

Mountain ranges like the Andes and the Himalayas may look everlasting, but they're actually just as vulnerable to climate change as any other biome. As glaciers melt and retreat from mountains, the rock warms up. Landslides and rockslides can thunder down the slopes. More intense storms caused by a warming atmosphere trigger deadly avalanches in areas with deep snowpack. Mountain rivers and waterfalls fill with melted snow, causing them to flood their banks in the valley communities below. The plants and animals that are specially adapted to freezing-cold temperatures and snow find that a warmer, greener mountain is too hot for survival.

These giants need our help. Reforestation is key to mountain range sustainability and can also help combat the effects of climate change. Almost 40 percent of all mountainous areas on Earth are covered with trees. When these forests are cut down, rock and soil are loosened, causing rockslides and erosion. Replanting trees that were cut down for timber or burned during wildfires helps keep the mountain ecosystem where it belongs, as well as reduces carbon dioxide from the atmosphere.

Plastics make their way onto mountains, too. Climbers have found fragments of plastic just below the summit of Mount Everest. Litter and plastic trash strewn around the mountain flanks pollutes the ground and water and harms alpine animals. Cutting back on our plastic use and cleaning up the existing plastic pollution helps. With a little effort, our mountains can stay clean, beautiful places for skiing, hiking, climbing, farming, herding, and fishing—and safe, healthy homes for the animals and plants who live there.

HOW YOU CAN HELP

Get out in those mountains! Hiking and camping are great ways to experience alpine beauty. Here're some tips to keep your hike and campsite clean and safe:

- You've heard it before: "Take nothing but photos. Leave nothing but footprints." The old advice is good advice! Leave flowers, stones, and plants alone. But do pack out all your trash—every scrap! You should even take your food scraps—apple cores, carrot tops, orange peels. Even these biodegradable bits can take up to two years to break down—that's two years of other campers and hikers eyeballing your banana peel.

- At your campsite, keep close track of your food. Animals are just waiting to take a big bite out of that peanut butter sandwich as soon as you head off for a potty break in the woods. If you're car-camping, shut your food in your car or RV at night. If you're backpacking, bring a sturdy bag and rope and hang your food from a branch well off the ground at night.

- Speaking of potty breaks, keep yours as clean and invisible as possible. For (ahem) solid deposits, pick a spot away from any paths and trails. With a small trowel or a sturdy stick, dig a hole at least several inches deep. Make your deposit, as it were, in the hole, and wipe with either a large leaf that you can identify (no poison ivy!) or plain white biodegradable toilet paper. Then bury the toilet paper and the poop completely, so that the hole is totally filled in. Tamp it down and scatter leaves on the top. Plant a large, upright stick in the hole so that no other hikers try to do their business in that spot.

One of the nice things in Minecraft is that I can carry a ton of stuff with no need for a bag. That's not so true on Earth, and this leads to many plastic bags being wasted. You might want to start carrying cloth bags to hold your things. They won't fit a furnace or 64 blocks of cobblestone, but they're great for groceries!

This quesadilla mixes some good old potatoes, some cheese (the wonders of what milk can be crafted into!), and chile peppers, which can be hot like the lava in the Nether. And there's those mashed potatoes again . . . so close to the baked potatoes I'm used to, but so much richer and creamier.

I've been thinking about the right Minecraft mashing tool, by the way, and I think a trident is out of the running.

POTATO AND CHILE QUESADILLA

You can really have fun with this recipe. Experiment with different cheeses or different chiles (or no chile), add cooked shredded chicken or sausage, and add canned beans or leftover cooked vegetables like corn, bell peppers, or zucchini. The mashed potato helps keep all of the ingredients from escaping from the tortilla!

Makes 1 quesadilla

INGREDIENTS

½ cup leftover mashed potatoes (see page 76)

1 tablespoon chopped scallions

½ teaspoon garlic powder or grated fresh garlic

½ cup shredded cheddar cheese

2 tablespoons canned diced green chiles (optional)

2 (10-inch) flour tortillas

1 tablespoon butter

1 tablespoon vegetable oil

DIRECTIONS

1. In a bowl, stir together the mashed potatoes, scallions, garlic powder, cheddar, and chiles (if using). Spread evenly over one of the tortillas, leaving about 1 inch of space around the edges. Top with the second tortilla.

2. In a large skillet, heat the butter and oil over medium heat until the butter is melted and sizzles. Carefully place the quesadilla in the skillet and cook for about 2 minutes. Peek underneath by lifting an edge with a spatula to make sure it's nicely browned, then flip carefully and brown on the other side for about another 2 minutes.

3. Slide the quesadilla out of the pan onto a cutting board and cut it into wedges to serve.

MASHED POTATOES

Here's an easy way to know how big a potato is: A small potato should fit easily in a child's hand, and a medium potato should fit easily in an adult's hand. There are about 2 medium potatoes in a pound.

Serves 4

INGREDIENTS

4 medium russet potatoes
2 teaspoons salt
1 cup milk
1 stick (4 ounces) butter
$^1/_2$ teaspoon ground white pepper

I wish I could mash potatoes in Minecraft instead of just eating them baked. What might be a good tool? A sword, a hoe, a shovel, an axe, or a trident? Hmm, I might have to get back to you on that. Luckily people on Earth have the right tools!

DIRECTIONS

1. Peel the potatoes, rinse, and cut into quarters. Place in a large saucepan and add enough cold water to cover. Add 1 teaspoon of the salt.

2. Bring to a boil, reduce the heat to medium, and simmer until tender, 30 to 40 minutes. Poke them with a fork to make sure they're super soft.

3. Meanwhile, in a small saucepan, heat the milk and butter until the butter melts and keep warm.

4. Drain the potatoes and return them to the saucepan over low heat. Add the milk/butter mixture a little at a time and mash with a potato masher or whip with an electric hand mixer. (DO NOT use a blender or food processor! This will make the mixture rubbery and you don't want that.)

5. Add the white pepper and the remaining 1 teaspoon salt. Remove from the heat and serve.

Here is another interesting potato recipe, and it comes with a history lesson. I hear that Naples, the place that this dish came from, is near a mountain called Vesuvius, which exploded many hundreds of years ago. I'm trying to imagine how huge that explosion must have been. I don't think even a creeper could compare.

DIRECTIONS

1. Preheat the oven to 375°F.

2. Rub the inside of an 8-inch round or square baking pan with 1 tablespoon of the oil or butter. In a small bowl, stir together the remaining 1 tablespoon oil or butter and the bread crumbs and set aside.

3. In a large bowl, combine the mashed potatoes, eggs, cheeses, and meats. Season with salt and pepper and stir everything together. Scrape into the prepared pan.

4. Top with the bread crumb mixture and bake until browned and bubbling, 25 to 30 minutes.

GATTÒ
(NEAPOLITAN POTATO AND CHEESE BAKE)

Gattò is the Neapolitan spelling of gâteau, meaning "cake" in French. A long time ago, Naples was ruled by France and that's when the name gattò came to be. This one is a creamy, cheesy, savory potato cake with a crunchy topping. You can really play around with this recipe, experimenting with different cheeses and meats (or no meat at all) and even chopped, cooked vegetables.

Serves 4 to 6

INGREDIENTS

2 tablespoons oil or butter

1/2 cup plain dried bread crumbs

3 cups mashed potatoes, left over or freshly made (see page 76), cooled

3 large eggs

1 cup shredded mozzarella, smoked mozzarella, or provolone cheese (or a combination)

1/2 cup grated parmesan cheese

1/2 cup chopped ham, salami, prosciutto, or mortadella (or a combination)

Salt and freshly ground black pepper

HASSELBACK POTATOES

The name Hasselback—and these potatoes—comes from a restaurant in Sweden. They look like little armadillos and turn out buttery and crunchy. If you like them loaded, top them with cooked broccoli, grated cheddar cheese, crumbled cooked bacon, chopped scallions, and/or sour cream or Greek yogurt.

Serves 4

INGREDIENTS

Softened butter, oil, or cooking spray for the baking sheet

4 medium potatoes, scrubbed well and dried

3 tablespoons butter

3 tablespoons vegetable oil (olive oil is good for this)

Flaky or kosher salt and freshly ground black pepper

I like a good campfire when exploring the mountains. So much room for cooking multiple things at a time, and no need to consume any fuel (not to mention how much it calms down my bees).

Be careful around the open flames if you do use a campfire, and enjoy your potatoes!

DIRECTIONS

1. Preheat the oven to 425°F. Line a baking sheet with foil or parchment and rub with a bit of butter or oil, or spray with cooking spray.

2. Working with one potato at a time, place it on a cutting board with the long side facing you, and lay 2 table knives or chopsticks along the length of the potato, one on each side, right up against the potato. This will keep your knife from slicing all the way through the potato. Now take a sharp knife and cut the potato crosswise into thin slices until you reach those knives. Cut all across the length of the potato. It should look like an armadillo but still be in one piece. Move it to the prepared baking sheet.

3. In a small saucepan, melt the butter and oil together and brush half of this onto the potatoes. Season with a sprinkling of salt and pepper.

4. Bake for 15 minutes. Brush with the remaining butter mixture and continue baking until the potatoes are tender and crispy when poked with a fork, another 15 minutes. If you're loading up your potatoes, add the cheese and bake for another few minutes, to melt.

VARIATION

Campfire Hasselbacks: To cook Hasselback potatoes in a campfire, follow the recipe for Hasselback Potatoes but wrap each potato individually in foil and add all of the butter or oil to the foil parcels. Cook on the grill or in the embers as directed in the oven recipe. Unwrap one of the potatoes after 30 minutes and test its doneness with a fork.

In my world, I've only got the one way of cooking meat. It can get a little same-y, I'll admit. But on Earth I'm seeing so many ways of preparing meats!

DIRECTIONS

1. First slice the chicken breasts horizontally to make 2 thin cutlets. To do this, hold a knife parallel to the cutting board and cut into the fatter side of the chicken breast, then slice all the way to the other side so you end up with thin cutlets. It doesn't matter if they aren't perfect; they'll be hidden under the bread crumbs anyway. Sprinkle both sides of the chicken with the salt and pepper.

2. Set up a dredging station in three shallow bowls: Place the flour in one bowl, the eggs in a second, and the bread crumbs in the third. Have a large plate or baking sheet ready. Dip both sides of each cutlet first in the flour, then the egg, then the bread crumbs, pressing to make sure the bread crumbs stick. Place them on the baking sheet.

3. In a large skillet, heat the oil over medium heat. To test the oil to make sure it's hot enough to fry, dip the handle of a wooden spoon into the oil. It's hot enough when the oil bubbles up around the handle. (That'll be 350° to 365°F on a thermometer.) Line a plate with paper towels. Working in batches so you don't crowd the pan (or the cutlets won't get as crispy), add 2 cutlets and cook until nicely browned on both sides, about 2 minutes on each side.

4. Drain them for a second on the paper towels before serving.

HOW TO MAKE A CRISPY CUTLET

You can't make a crispy cutlet without a crispy coating. This recipe uses plain dried bread crumbs, but you could also use panko bread crumbs, crushed pretzels, or crushed cornflakes.

Serves 4

INGREDIENTS

2 large boneless, skinless chicken breasts

1 teaspoon salt

$1/2$ teaspoon freshly ground black pepper

$1/2$ cup all-purpose flour

2 large eggs, stirred with a fork to combine

$1 1/2$ cups plain dried bread crumbs

$1/2$ cup vegetable oil

KATSU WITH CURRY SAUCE

Katsu means "cutlets" in Japanese, and when made with pork they are called tonkatsu.

Serves 4

INGREDIENTS

CURRY SAUCE

1 medium onion, cut into chunks

1 large carrot, peeled and cut into chunks

1 large potato, peeled and cut into chunks

1 garlic clove, grated

2 tablespoons ketchup

2 tablespoons soy sauce

1 tablespoon sugar

1 teaspoon salt

2 cups water

3 tablespoons butter

3 tablespoons all-purpose flour

1 to 2 tablespoons mild curry powder, to taste

CUTLETS

4 boneless pork loin chops

1 teaspoon salt

1/2 teaspoon freshly ground black pepper

1/2 cup all-purpose flour

2 large eggs, stirred with a fork to combine

1 1/2 cups panko bread crumbs

1/2 cup vegetable oil

> Katsu are made with different meats, and this time around it's with pork, one of my favorites! I've spent more emeralds than I care to admit on butchers' porkchop stocks....

DIRECTIONS

1. **Make the curry sauce:** In a large saucepan, stir together the onion, carrot, potato, garlic, ketchup, soy sauce, sugar, salt, and water and bring to a boil. Reduce to a simmer and cook until the vegetables are tender, about 15 minutes. Turn off the heat and keep warm.

2. In a large skillet or Dutch oven, melt the butter over medium heat and mix in the flour with a wire whisk. Cook and stir until the mixture is bubbling, 2 or 3 minutes.

3. With a wire whisk, add the curry powder and stir for another minute. Whisk in about a cup of the warm cooking water at a time, allowing it to bubble up and thicken between additions. You can reduce the heat if it sputters. Continue adding the water until the sauce is as thick as you like. Now stir in the cooked vegetables.

4. **Let's make the cutlets:** Working one at a time, sandwich a porkchop between two pieces of plastic wrap and flatten slightly by pounding with a meat mallet. If you don't have a mallet, then a rubber mallet, rolling pin, or small heavy skillet will do. Sprinkle both sides of the meat with the salt and pepper.

5. Set up a dredging station in three shallow bowls: Place the flour in one, the eggs in a second, and the panko in the third. Have a large plate or baking sheet ready. Dip both sides of each cutlet first in the flour, then the egg, then the panko, pressing to make sure the panko sticks. Place on the baking sheet.

6. In a large skillet, heat the oil over medium heat. To test the oil to make sure it's hot enough to fry, dip the handle of a wooden spoon into the oil. It's hot enough when the oil bubbles up around the handle. (That'll be 350° to 365°F on a thermometer.)

7. Line a plate with paper towels. Working in batches so you don't crowd the pan (or the cutlets won't get as crispy), add the cutlets to the pan and cook until nicely browned, about 2 minutes on each side. Drain them for a second on the paper towels.

8. Pour the curry sauce on top of the cooked cutlets and serve.

I never knew bread crumbs had so many uses. I tend to make a lot of crumbs whenever I eat.... Maybe I should try collecting some for this recipe.

SWEET SOY KOREAN-STYLE FRIED CHICKEN

Start this the day before you plan to eat it.

You'll need a deep-fry thermometer for this recipe. It's the double frying at different temperatures that helps make this extra crunchy.

Serves 4

INGREDIENTS

Oil for deep-frying (peanut oil is best, but canola oil is good, too)

1 cup potato starch

8 chicken drumsticks or 12 wings

SAUCE

1 cup packed light brown sugar or honey

1 tablespoon cornstarch

1/2 cup soy sauce

2 tablespoons unseasoned rice vinegar

3 tablespoons freshly squeezed orange juice (about 1/2 orange)

2 cloves garlic, grated

1 teaspoon grated fresh ginger

2 teaspoons toasted sesame oil

A few dashes of red pepper flakes (optional, if you like it spicy)

> This recipe calls for the food to be fried, which I think is a little different from watching zombies and other mobs fry in the first light of dawn.

DIRECTIONS

1. Pour 1 inch oil into a deep heavy-bottomed pan or deep-fryer and bring it to 300°F on a deep-fry thermometer.

2. Meanwhile, put a wire rack on a baking sheet.

3. Put the potato starch in a paper or plastic bag and shake each piece of chicken in it to coat. Working in two batches so you don't crowd the pan, fry the chicken in the hot oil for about 5 minutes on each side. It will be cooked but not fully browned. (It's important to keep the oil at 300°F.) Set the fried chicken on the rack and cool completely. When the chicken is completely cool, wrap it in plastic wrap and freeze it for at least 6 hours or overnight.

4. Strain the oil to remove the bits and return it to the pan. Cover and save for the next day.

5. The next day, remove the chicken from the freezer and unwrap it about 1 hour before you plan to cook it.

6. Make the sauce: In a small saucepan over medium heat, stir together the brown sugar and cornstarch. Stir in the soy sauce, vinegar, orange juice, garlic, ginger, sesame oil, and pepper flakes (if using). Bring to a boil, stirring until it thickens slightly. Pour the sauce into a large bowl and keep it warm while you cook the chicken.

7. Add enough fresh oil to what's left in the deep fryer so it comes up to 1 inch. Heat it over medium heat to 350°F on a deep-fry thermometer. (Or use the wooden spoon trick to test the temperature from the How to Make a Crispy Cutlet recipe, page 83.)

8. Again working in two batches, fry the chicken until nicely browned, 6 to 8 minutes per side, turning once. As it's done, move it to the rack while you fry the rest.

9. When all the chicken is done, add it to the bowl of sauce and toss it to coat. Serve hot.

JUNGLES

It's almost impossible to talk about Earth's rainforest and jungle biomes without big words. The oldest living ecosystem on Earth! Houses more than half of all the world's plant and animal species! Dense, green, layered, humid, packed with life from the top of the canopy to the creeping critters under the soil. Our tropical forests, such as the Amazon, are the most ecologically diverse systems on the planet. This means that a staggering variety of plants and animals are found there—and not just existing, but packed into every bit of space. Just 4 quare miles of rainforest might contain 750 different species of trees and 150 different species of butterflies.

Our jungles also have unique mobs and plants! I can find ocelots, which are great at keeping creepers away, and parrots, which I can tame with seeds. I also love to collect cocoa pods so I can get cocoa beans for my cookies. And melons are a special treat found in the jungle, too! I'm thrilled to learn that people also like cocoa and melons on Earth. In fact, we have some special recipes in this section dedicated to them.

Because it's near the equator, the Amazon rainforest—Earth's largest tropical forest—is warm and wet. All of the trees and plants keep it green, and the rainforest makes about 75 percent of its own rain just from evaporation. Meanwhile, monkeys climb through the trees, boa snakes hang from branches as they wait for a meal to pass by, and eagles wheel overhead while parrots flash from treetop to treetop. Jaguars stalk silently through the brush, while in the rivers, caimans hunt fish.

The jungle is a special biome, and it's also under special threats. Vast swaths of Amazon rainforest are being cut to the ground and burned to make room for farms and ranches. Companies log trees for timber and dig mines to extract valuable ores, like gold. The rainforest is disappearing, and with it the incredible plants and animals that make their home there—some of which are species we've never even seen.

Jungle is often cleared using fire, and when it burns it releases millions of tons of stored carbon dioxide into the atmosphere. Smoke from the fires pollutes the surrounding land. The burned land can no longer collect and store carbon dioxide, removing it from the atmosphere. At a certain point, the Amazon rainforest will begin to dry up, and the cycle of wetness and evaporation that keeps it green will be broken.

HOW YOU CAN HELP

Put your money where your mouth is! Buying low-impact foods and reading labels carefully can help turn your grocery shopping into an ethical adventure.

■ Some countries that have tropical forests within their borders are working to end deforestation. We can help, too. Much of the land is being cleared for beef production. By choosing not to eat or buy beef or buying sustainably produced beef, we can show our support for the jungle biome. Experiment with making your favorite recipes vegetarian by substituting beans or vegan meat alternatives.

■ Bring your own reusable bags and skip the plastic! Single-use plastic like grocery bags is a giant contributor to worldwide plastic pollution and the production of these plastics just adds to the greenhouse gas burden—none of which is good for our tropical forests.

■ Look for local, organic produce, if you can. Locally grown means less time on fossil-fuel guzzling trucks and tanker ships. Organic means few pesticides sprayed into the ground and water system. And try to choose produce that's in-season in your area, too! Root vegetables in the winter, if you live in a cold place, and cherries in the summer. Eating cherries during a northern winter means those puppies have spent a lot of time on a ship—one that most likely runs on fossil fuels!

■ Choose products that have the least amount of packaging, and when you can, choose paper and glass over plastic. These materials aren't perfect, but they're more sustainable than plastic in almost every case. And always choose the product with packaging that has the highest percentage of recyclable content. Are you in a store that allows you to bring your own containers? Do it! Reusing containers is the best way to cut down on nonsustainable packaging.

In the Overworld, cows are always nearby if you explore a little bit. But that's not the case for a lot of people on Earth. On the other hand, you probably don't need to prepare their meat yourself. Your town might have a local meat market, which is more sustainable than the big stores that ship from far away. It can also support local people, and it's easier to make sure the animals are being properly taken care of.

HOW TO MAKE
FRESH SALSA

This is sometimes called pico de gallo, which means "beak of rooster." You could imagine a rooster pecking away at all the ingredients to chop them into tiny pieces—which is what you'll do to make this. (Without the beak!)

Makes about 2 cups

INGREDIENTS

2 medium tomatoes

⅓ cup chopped red onion

½ to 1 small jalapeño or serrano chile, seeded and finely chopped

2 tablespoons chopped fresh cilantro

Juice of 1 lime

½ teaspoon salt

"Beak of rooster," huh? Y'know, first time I learned about roosters, I thought someone had just splashed dye on a chicken. Then I found out they make noises like no chicken I've ever heard before!

I don't think I'd trust one of those guys to chop my tomatoes up. You'll do a much better job by hand.

DIRECTIONS

Halve the tomatoes and remove the seeds. Chop the tomatoes and add the onion, chile, cilantro, lime juice, and salt. Stir together and serve very fresh. If making ahead, don't add the cilantro until just before serving.

FRUIT SAL

Makes about

INGRE
1 s

...LSA

...2 cups

...IENTS

...up chopped fresh fruit

1 cup chopped tomato

1/3 cup chopped red onion or scallion

1/2 to 1 hot red chile, such as jalapeño, Fresno, or cayenne, seeded and finely chopped

2 tablespoons chopped fresh cilantro, basil, or mint (or a combination)

Grated zest and juice of 1 lime

1/2 teaspoon kosher salt

This salsa is going to take one of my favorite foods from the jungle—melon—and mix it up with lots of Earth ingredients I'm not so familiar with, like mint. This is definitely a new way for me to experience this jungle fruit! Before, I thought it was just fancy to break open a melon and have it in slices. On Earth, it seems mint has been used for a long time to help people's stomachs feel better, so I wonder what would happen if I add a little mint to a potion of Healing?

DIRECTIONS

In a bowl, stir together the fruit, tomato, onion, chile, cilantro, lime zest, lime juice, and salt. This salsa is best eaten very fresh. To make ahead, add the herbs just before serving.

VARIATIONS

Using the base recipe, change up the fruit and herb combinations. Here are a few suggestions, but then get creative with your own fruit and herb combos.

Pineapple + mint or cilantro

Mango + cilantro + basil

Plum + basil + mint

Strawberry + basil

Peach + basil + cilantro

Lots of Earth cooking involves roots, I'm finding out. I'm very used to roots, whether mangrove roots or hanging roots on the roofs of lush caves, but I wouldn't want to eat them! Mind you, this dish looks a lot better to eat than a plate of hanging roots does!

DIRECTIONS

1. Peel the mangoes with a vegetable peeler, then cut the flesh into little cubes. (There will be a big pit in the center. Throw it away.) Put the cubes in a large bowl.

2. Peel the cucumber and halve it lengthwise. Use a small spoon to scoop out the seeds and cut the cucumber into little cubes. Add them to the bowl.

3. The jicama skin can be woody and tough. You may have to peel it with a paring knife, then cut the flesh into little cubes. Add it to the bowl. If you are using radishes, trim off the greens, then wash the radishes and cut them into quarters.

4. In a small bowl, stir together the lime juice, oil, $1/2$ teaspoon of the salt, and the honey. Add this to the bowl with the fruit and stir together well. In a little cup, stir together the remaining $1/2$ teaspoon salt and the chile powder. Sprinkle this onto the salad just before serving.

MANGO, JICAMA, AND CUCUMBER SALAD

On street corners in Mexico, vendors cut up mangoes, jicama, and cucumber and sell them in little cups, dusted with a seasoning called Tajín (say "tah-HEEN") that contains salt, chile powder, and powdered lime juice. Here, we've turned them into a refreshing sweet/salty/tart salad.

Serves 4

INGREDIENTS

2 large mangoes

1 small jicama root or a handful of radishes

1 medium cucumber

Juice of 2 limes

1 tablespoon canola oil

1 teaspoon salt

1 teaspoon honey

1 teaspoon mild or hot chile powder

A jungle means lots of trees and plants, and some might offer up fruit to eat. For this recipe, we're going way past the melons you find in a Minecraft jungle and dishing up all kinds of fruit. It's important people on Earth eat enough fruit every day to restore their hunger points. . . . I mean, to have a healthy and balanced diet.

DIRECTIONS

In a blender or food processor, combine the frozen fruit, milk, sweetener, and chia seeds and blend until smooth. Scrape into bowls and top with whatever toppings you like.

HOW TO MAKE A
MORNING
BOWL

Acai is the (super!) fruit of a palm tree that grows in Brazil. It's the original morning bowl fruit, but you can use lots of others. It might be difficult to find fresh acai fruit in some areas, but you can get it frozen in little packets in many supermarkets.

Serves 3 to 4

INGREDIENTS

1 cup frozen chopped fruit, such as acai, peach, mango, pineapple, berries, or banana (or a combination)

½ cup milk of any kind (coconut, almond, oat, hemp, or rice)

1 tablespoon liquid sweetener (agave, maple syrup, or honey)

2 teaspoons chia seeds

TOPPINGS

Chopped fresh fruit

Dried fruit (raisins, craisins, mango, papaya, or dates)

Coconut, shredded or flaked

Nuts (walnuts, pecans, pistachios, almonds, peanuts, or cashews)

Cacao nibs

Chocolate chips

Banana chips

Granola

Bee pollen

ROASTED SWEET PLANTAINS

In Latin American and Caribbean countries, sweet plantains are eaten alongside beans and rice the way North Americans and Europeans eat sweet potatoes with lunch or dinner. There are green (unripe) plantains, which are starchy like potatoes and best fried. When the skin of a plantain has turned black and the fruit soft, it's at its sweetest and becomes caramelized when fried. Yellow plantains are somewhere in between: sweet but not too sweet.

Serves 4 to 6

INGREDIENTS

8 tablespoons (1 stick/4 ounces) salted butter, at room temperature

2 tablespoons honey

1/2 teaspoon ground cinnamon, plus more for sprinkling

1/4 cup fresh lime juice (about 2 limes)

4 yellow plantains

Plantains are a lot like that other Earth fruit, bananas. They're long like a sword, but these look much too soft to use for sword work, even if yellow plantains might look a teensy bit like golden swords. Would it be a bad joke if I replaced someone's golden sword with a plantain? I'd give back the golden sword, of course, and offer this recipe with my apologies.

DIRECTIONS

1. Preheat the oven to 400°F.

2. Lightly grease a 9 × 13-inch baking pan with 1 tablespoon of the butter.

3. In a small saucepan over medium heat, melt the remaining 7 tablespoons butter. Remove it from the heat and whisk in the honey, cinnamon, and lime juice until smooth.

4. Prepare the plantains by removing one strip of the peel, exposing the plantain. With your fingers, loosen the rest of the peel from the flesh while keeping the plantain intact and leaving the peel in place. Place flesh-side up in the prepared baking pan (if they topple over, slice a little bit off the underside to create a flat area for the plantain to sit on).

5. With a pastry brush, brush half of the butter mixture evenly over the top of each plantain, letting it drip down into the loosened peel.

6. Bake for 15 minutes. Brush with the remaining butter mixture and continue to bake until the plantains are browned and tender when you poke them with a fork, another 15 to 20 minutes.

7. Sprinkle with a bit more cinnamon before serving.

I was so impressed to learn that hominy has been harvested by Indigenous people in North America for ten thousand years! Since days in my world take up much less time than Earth days, this is a huge number for me to wrap my head around. Maybe after I eat some of this delicious food I can do the math to figure out how many Minecraft days would span ten thousand Earth years.

DIRECTIONS

In a large pot, combine the broth, salsa, hominy, romaine, and chicken (if using). Cover and simmer over medium heat for 20 minutes. Serve in bowls with whichever toppings you like.

TOPPING IDEAS

Chopped fresh cilantro

Sliced radishes

Chopped onion or scallions

Avocado chunks

Shredded lettuce or cabbage

Tortilla chips

Pickled jalapeño slices

Shredded Jack cheese or parmesan cheese

Sour cream

Lime wedges, for squeezing

GREEN POZOLE

Pozole is both the name of this stew as well as the Spanish word for hominy, which are the chewy, fluffy corn kernels that tortillas and grits are made of. This super-easy pozole gets its green color in part from cooked lettuce. That might sound strange, but it cooks just like spinach or kale and is sweet and mild.

Serves 4

INGREDIENTS

1 quart chicken broth

1 cup store-bought tomatillo salsa

1 (29-ounce) can hominy, drained

2 cups chopped romaine lettuce or escarole (wilted outer leaves are good for this!) or a big handful of baby spinach

Optional: Shredded cooked chicken or leftover pork from Cuban Pork (page 46)

Toppings (see Topping Ideas, at left)

DESERTS

Deserts. Hot. Dry. Perhaps someone staggering through sand dunes, a palm tree mirage in the distance. True? Sort of. Desert biomes are dry. That's what makes them desert. "Arid," to use a fancy word for "not a whole lot of water around here."

Desert biomes cover about one-fifth of the Earth's land surface and they're not all the sand dune variety. Some deserts in North America, Europe, and Greenland are semi-arid. Shrubby plants and small trees can grow in the rocky soil, and they get some rain, just not a lot. Picture some parts of Utah—sagebrush and cacti—that's semiarid. "Cold deserts" are a confusing oxymoron, kind of like "jumbo shrimp." But they're a thing. Antarctica is the most famous cold desert biome. The icy, rocky continent is covered with snow and ice that is permanent. It actually doesn't get a whole lot of actual precipitation, which makes it a desert.

The Mohave sounds like the kind of desert I'm familiar with—hot, sandy, and full of spiky cacti. I like to find desert villages out there so that I don't get lonely, and plenty of people on Earth live in deserts, too!

The Sahara Desert on the African continent is one of the most famous hot-dry-sandy varieties. So is the Mohave in the American Southwest. In the Sinai Desert in North Africa and the Arabian Desert in the Middle East, dunes and dry yellow and white sand stretch for miles.

Plants and animals that make their homes in the desert know how to handle this whole "very little rain" situation. Plants like cacti have big stems to store water. Tough plants like sagebrush need very little moisture to live. Their shiny leaves reflect light, so they don't absorb too much sun. Camels can drink huge amounts of water at one time, then store it in their bloodstream, allowing them to go long periods of time with no water at all. (They don't store water in their humps, despite what people think. Camels' humps are made of fat, which they use for energy when food is scarce.) Small desert rodents burrow under the soil or sand during the day to avoid the heat and save moisture in their bodies.

Deserts are surprisingly delicate biomes. Every plant and animal on the land is specially adapted to the balance of water and dryness around it. Climate change is making some desert biomes even drier, shriveling up even the plants that need very little moisture. People who graze too many animals on the land or cut down small trees and shrubs for firewood are making this problem worse. Soil erodes or blows away. Animals lose their habitats. And areas that were already desert grow even larger.

But desert biomes can be protected just like any other. Controlling the number of grazing animals on desert land helps. Helping people find alternatives to cutting desert firewood keeps plants and trees where they belong. Replanting native shrubs and trees keeps the soil on the ground, not swirled away on the wind.

Living in a desert biome? Cutting back on water use helps keep desert waterways full. We've all heard it before—take short showers instead of baths, install low-flow toilet flushers, plant a desert-native lawn and garden—but these things work! By taking less water for ourselves, our animals, and our plants, we can make sure the desert biome's delicate water-land balance is preserved.

HOW YOU CAN HELP

Water is a scarce resource in desert environments. But we can save water wherever we live. A rain barrel can be a great way to keep your garden wet with the free, sustainable water that falls from the sky—rain!

A rain barrel is a large drum, usually made of plastic. Put it under a downspout (that's the open pipe that leads from your house gutters to the ground). The rain flows from the downspout into the barrel and collects it. There's a spigot at the bottom. Just open the spigot and you can use the rainwater to water your garden. In some climates, you can save over a thousand gallons of water just by using a rain barrel!

Ready for rain-barreling? Look for a big one. A good rain barrel is between 50 and 80 gallons. You also might need an adult with a hacksaw or other kind of saw to cut into your downspout. (Leave this job to a grown-up. It's a little tricky). Find a garden hose, too, and make sure it fits the spigot at the bottom of the rain barrel.

You're ready to set up! Roll the barrel up near the downspout you're going to use. Get the adult-with-the-saw and stand back. They'll cut the downspout so it fits down into the hole at the top of the barrel. Then attach the hose to the spigot at the bottom. That's it! It's so simple! Rain will flow from your house gutters, into the downspout, then into the barrel. When you turn the spigot, the water in the rain barrel will gust into the hose. Now get watering and pat yourself on the back for doing your part to save precious water.

It's tricky to grow plants in the deserts of the Overworld. You have to bring dirt because most plants can't grow in sand, and find water to use to irrigate. We don't have to worry about heat and water evaporating, though, so it's even more impressive to see the amazing ways Earth people can make deserts their homes!

HOW TO MAKE
YOGURT

Yogurt is traditionally made in places that are very hot, and where milk goes sour quickly. Yogurt lasts longer than fresh milk, is super healthy, and you can make all sorts of yummy things with it.

Makes 1 quart

INGREDIENTS

1 quart whole or 2% milk

4 tablespoons plain yogurt with active cultures (store-bought or saved from a batch you've made yourself), at room temperature

In Minecraft, I can take a fermented spider eye and use it to make potions. On Earth, I see that people can take milk and use bacterial fermentation on it to make yogurt! I've learned that yogurt ferments thanks to the natural sugars in milk. I guess that's why spider eyes require sugar added to ferment.... They don't seem very sweet on their own.

You might not be able to make a potion out of yogurt, but just like milk in Minecraft, it has a lot of health benefits.

DIRECTIONS

1. Pour the milk into a heavy-bottomed saucepan over medium-low heat and very slowly bring it up to a simmer. You should just see little bubbles forming around the edges of the pan and the milk will begin to steam. If you use a thermometer, you're looking for 200°F. Stir the milk from time to time while it's heating so the bottom doesn't stick.

2. Remove the pan from the heat and let the milk cool to body temperature, or about 100°F if you use a thermometer. You can test the temperature by carefully putting a drop on your inside wrist. You shouldn't be able to feel that it's hot or cold.

3. If the milk has formed a skin on top, remove it and eat it as a cook's treat sprinkled with a bit of sugar. (But do this later. We have yogurt to make!) With a wire whisk, stir in the yogurt and combine it very, very, VERY well.

4. Cover the pot and wrap it entirely (swaddle it!) in a heavy bath towel or a couple of layers of thick kitchen towel and put it in the warmest spot of your kitchen where it won't be disturbed. On top of the fridge is good (heat rises) or inside the oven with only the light turned on. Leave it for at least 12 hours. The longer it sits, the thicker and more tart it becomes.

5. Whisk the yogurt to combine any whey that's separated and transfer to another container to store in the fridge. Save a bit of this batch to start your next batch!

GREEK YOGURT AND LABNEH

Makes 2 cups Greek yogurt
or 1 1/2 cups labneh

INGREDIENT

**1 quart Homemade Yogurt
(page 106)**

I've discovered that while labneh looks like yogurt, it's actually a cheese. Phew! There's a lot of variety in foods on Earth! Labneh is a really popular thing to eat in a place called the Middle East, where I can see on the map there is a lot of desert. And people who live in the desert full-time are going to be really good at making food with spare resources, as well as coming up with ways to make foods last longer in hot climates—like turning milk into cheese.

DIRECTIONS

1. Line a large sturdy sieve all the way up the sides with two layers of paper towels, paper coffee filters, or cheesecloth. Set the sieve over a deep bowl or pot. (Alternatively, line a colander and set it on a wire rack set over the bowl or pot.) Cover the sieve (or colander) and put the whole operation in the fridge.

2. For Greek yogurt, let it drain for 2 hours. For labneh, which is thick enough to spread, drain it for 4 to 6 hours.

YES, WHEY!

The liquid that drains from the yogurt is called whey. DO NOT throw this away. It's full of good-for-you things! You can use it in place of milk in smoothies or morning bowls instead of water to make lemonade, as a replacement for buttermilk or water in baking and in pancakes and waffles, and instead of water to make salt-fermented pickles and brine for brining poultry and meat!

These cucumbers look a bit like sea pickles, but they don't light up. Good thing you don't have to go underwater to find them!

YOGURT AND CUCUMBERS

The mix of yogurt with cucumbers is found in many countries where the weather is hot and the food is spicy. Here is the basic recipe with variations to make the South Asian (raita), Greek (tzatziki), and Turkish (caçik) versions.

Makes 2 cups

INGREDIENTS

2 cups plain yogurt, store-bought or homemade (see page 106)

1 small cucumber, peeled, seeded, and chopped

1/2 teaspoon salt

1 fat clove garlic, grated

DIRECTIONS

Mix the yogurt, cucumber, salt, and garlic and refrigerate.

VARIATIONS

Raita: Follow the recipe for Yogurt and Cucumbers. In a dry skillet, toast 2 teaspoons cumin seeds or ground cumin over medium heat, stirring, until browned and smelling toasty, about 2 minutes for the powder and 5 minutes for the seeds. Let cool, then crush the seeds between your fingers. Stir the toasted cumin into the yogurt. Serve chilled.

Tzatziki: Follow the recipe for Yogurt and Cucumbers and stir in 2 tablespoons chopped fresh dill and 1 tablespoon olive oil.

Caçik: Follow the recipe for Yogurt and Cucumbers and stir in 1 tablespoon dried mint, 2 tablespoons olive oil, and 2 tablespoons cold water.

HOW TO MAKE
LENTIL SOUP

Lentils are one of the few pulses (the group that includes chickpeas, beans, and dried peas) that cook quickly without having to be soaked.

In Italy, lentils are eaten on New Year's Day for good luck, because they are shaped like coins.

Serves 4 to 6

INGREDIENTS

4 tablespoons olive oil or ghee

2 medium onions, chopped

2 medium carrots, peeled and chopped

2 stalks celery, chopped

3 fat cloves garlic, chopped

1 large potato, peeled and cut into small cubes

2 cups brown or green lentils, rinsed

2 bay leaves

2 quarts chicken or vegetable broth

1 cup water, whey, or tomato juice

Salt and freshly ground black pepper

I'm only just realizing now that lentils are actually seeds! I've never eaten a seed before, but the chickens in my yard certainly enjoy them. Looking at this recipe I can see why. It's so interesting to see the different forms a thing like a seed can take in your world.

DIRECTIONS

1. In a large pot, heat the olive oil over medium-high heat. Add the onions, carrots, celery, and garlic and cook, stirring, until they soften and begin to brown, about 8 minutes.

2. Stir in the potato, lentils, bay leaves, broth, water, 1 generous teaspoon salt, and pepper to taste. Bring to a boil. Stir, reduce the heat, and boil gently until the lentils are very soft, about 45 minutes. Stir from time to time while the soup is cooking.

3. To make it thicker, puree just a small portion of it right in the pot with a stick blender or blend about a cupful in a regular blender and return it to the pot.

VARIATIONS

Curry Coconut Lentil Soup: Follow the recipe for Basic Lentil Soup with these changes: When sautéing the vegetables, add 2 to 3 teaspoons mild curry powder. Substitute 1 sweet potato for the potato. Use red lentils. Reduce the chicken broth by 1 cup, omit the water, and add 2 cups canned coconut milk. The rest is the same. This is good served with a dollop of yogurt stirred through.

Moroccan-ish Lentil Soup: Follow the recipe for Basic Lentil Soup with these changes: When sautéing the vegetables, add 1 1/2 teaspoons ground turmeric, 1 teaspoon ground cumin, 1/2 teaspoon ground ginger, and 1/2 teaspoon ground cinnamon. Omit the potato and add 1 cup chickpeas in its place. Use French Puy lentils. Add 1 bunch cilantro, leaves only, during the last 10 minutes of cooking. The rest is the same. Just before serving, squeeze in the juice of 1 lemon. This is good served with a drizzle of extra olive oil on top.

> I might craft food on a campfire or in a furnace or a smoker, but a tandoor is new to me. Good thing it's only shaped like a beehive and isn't actually one. Cooking a beehive wouldn't end well!

YOGURT-MARINATED TANDOORI-ISH CHICKEN

Authentic tandoori chicken is cooked in a clay oven called a tandoor that looks like an upside-down beehive.

Serves 4 to 6

INGREDIENTS

3 pounds bone-in, skinless chicken breasts and leg quarters

Juice of 1/2 large lemon

1 1/2 teaspoons mild chile powder

2 teaspoons sweet paprika

1 teaspoon salt

MARINADE

1/2 cup plain yogurt

1/4 cup olive oil

Juice of 1/2 large lemon

2 fat cloves garlic, grated

1-inch piece fresh ginger, peeled and grated

2 teaspoons mild chile powder

1 1/2 teaspoons ground coriander

1 teaspoon ground cumin

1 1/2 teaspoons salt

1/2 teaspoon freshly ground black pepper

TO FINISH

4 tablespoons butter, melted

Lemon wedges

Raita (page 109)

DIRECTIONS

1. Pat the chicken dry. Cut deep slits in the flesh with a sharp knife, about 1 inch apart.

2. In a small bowl, combine the lemon juice, chile powder, paprika, and salt. Rub into the chicken, making sure you get the rub into the slits. Set the chicken aside on a plate while you make the marinade.

3. **Make the marinade:** In a large bowl, stir together the yogurt, olive oil, lemon juice, garlic, ginger, chile powder, coriander, cumin, salt, and pepper. Add the chicken to the bowl and mix very well to make sure all the chicken pieces are evenly coated. Cover and refrigerate for at least 2 hours or overnight.

4. Preheat the oven to 400°F.

5. **To finish:** Place a wire rack in a sheet pan and brush the rack with a bit of the melted butter. Remove the chicken from the bowl along with any marinade that sticks to it and place the pieces on the rack, flesh-side down. Roast for 30 minutes.

6. Turn the pieces over, brush with the rest of the melted butter, and roast until cooked through, another 15 to 20 minutes. The juices should run clear when pierced with a fork at the thickest point.

7. Serve with the lemon wedges and raita.

SWEET MOROCCAN-STYLE CARROT SALAD

Carrots are often cooked with orange and lemon juice, and spices like cumin, coriander, and paprika. Here, we've left them raw and lightly spiced.

Serves 4

INGREDIENTS

DRESSING

Grated zest of ½ lemon

Juice of ½ lemon

Grated zest of ¼ orange

Juice of 1 orange

1 tablespoon honey

½ teaspoon ground coriander

½ teaspoon ground cumin

¼ teaspoon ground cinnamon

½ teaspoon paprika

½ teaspoon salt

¼ teaspoon freshly ground black pepper

3 tablespoons olive oil

SALAD

3 tablespoons golden raisins

1 (10-ounce) package shredded carrots, or 6 medium carrots, peeled and shredded

⅓ cup fresh cilantro or mint, finely chopped

¼ cup roasted pistachios, chopped

I've ridden pigs by putting a saddle on them and then holding a carrot on a stick over the pig's head. It works every time! I'm trying to figure out how I can hook a salad to a stick. It might be a little tricky, but the taste is so good I think it will make a pig go even faster than it would for a regular carrot!

DIRECTIONS

1. **Make the dressing:** In a medium bowl, whisk together the lemon zest, lemon juice, orange zest, orange juice, and honey. Whisk in the spices, salt, and pepper. Finally, whisk in the olive oil, a little at a time.

2. **For the salad:** Add the raisins to the dressing, cover, and refrigerate until the raisins have plumped a bit, about 30 minutes.

3. Add the carrots to the bowl with the dressing and raisins and mix with tongs or a large spoon. Sprinkle with the cilantro and pistachios just before serving.

SWAMPS

Swamp biomes aren't water and they aren't land. They're something in between. These wetlands are spots of land that are always filled with water, either fresh or salt. They're found on every continent on Earth except Antarctica, and they can be as tiny as a splotch on the plains or they can stretch for miles.

Unlike some wetlands, swamps are filled with trees, which anchor down the muddy soil with their roots. Some swamps are named after the trees that live there, like cypress swamps or mangrove swamps.

This rich, wet, muddy biome is perfect as a home for ducks, otters, frogs, toads, crabs, crayfish, salamanders, and alligators. Some species swim into swamps from the ocean, lay their eggs in the quiet, protected waters, then swim back out again. Birds like egrets, herons, vultures, eagles, and hawks fish and hunt in the swamp while their droppings fertilize the waters.

I like to search swamps for pretty blue orchids and lily pads, as well as watch those hopping frogs chow down on some slime. They seem to find slime tasty, but I'd rather make something sweet with the sugar cane found here!

Water and flooding often carve out saltwater swamps along ocean coastlines. Tall, skinny trees called mangroves can fill these swamp waters. The roots that poke up above the water are called "knees." Others are filled with needle trees, like spruce or fir. Some freshwater swamps, like the Everglades in Florida, are actually giant rivers that move very slowly.

People have sometimes thought of swamps as creepy, mysterious places. Tales about eerie lights in swamps or ghosts fill the pages of storybooks. Or people have thought of the swamp biome as worthless land that is filled with pests, like mosquitoes—and there are often a lot of mosquitoes in swamps. Governments and some farmers would drain swampland to make it drier for building and agriculture. Almost half of the swamps in the United States were drained and filled in before the 1970s.

But swamps are actually incredibly important biomes that can protect people and their homes and buildings. Along coastlines, swamps act like giant sponges that can soak up the water that rushes inland. They help anchor land that might be washed away in storm surges. And swamps are pollutant scrubbers, too. The water-loving plants can absorb runoff from agriculture or factories. The swamp plants use some of the chemicals, like nitrogen. Others sink to the bottom of the swamp and are buried in the mud there.

We can help protect wetlands like swamps. People who are building homes or new businesses near swamplands can preserve them, instead of draining and filling. Swamps and other wetlands also store the carbon that keeps adding to climate change. Drain or destroy these delicate biomes and that carbon gets released into the atmosphere—just where we don't want it. Protect them and we help protect our planet—and ourselves.

HOW YOU CAN HELP

Swamps are a lot of things—wet, funky, maybe a little scary—and really fun to explore. With just a few tips, you can keep your swamp visit safe for both you and the biome around you.

■ Bring a plastic bag with you. With your guide's permission, you can pick up bits of trash and litter that you see. Just keep your hands out of the water—you don't want any animals mistaking your fingers for lunch.

■ Swamps are watery! Stay on the boardwalk or walkway, if there is one, even if the ground looks so close and so solid. You risk getting stuck or drowning by leaving the marked walkway. And swamps are delicate. You don't want to trample a nest or disturb eggs. If you're touring a swamp in a canoe or a kayak, stay in your boat. Your guide will know safe places to paddle.

■ Do your own bird and mammal count. Look around you and keep track of how many different types of animals and insects you see. Write down the numbers if you can. You'll be amazed at the biodiversity of the swamp biome.

■ Wear lots of bug spray, long pants, and long sleeves. Mosquitoes love the still, murky water of a swamp as much as other creatures. They'll also love you!

Wow, look at the great work swamps do . . . and you don't have to deal with dangerous witch huts or slimes in yours!

HOW TO COOK A POT OF BEANS

Here's how you cook beans the simplest way, with just a pot, water, and heat. One pound (2 cups) of dried beans yields about 6 cups of cooked beans. If your recipe calls for one 15-ounce can of beans, use a generous 1½ cups of cooked beans, drained. There are two steps to cooking dried beans and here they are!

1. SOAKING THE BEANS

Soaking the beans first allows them to absorb some water and cook faster. Beans double in size while they're soaking, so be sure to use a large enough pot and enough water. (Note: lentils, split peas, and black-eyed peas do not need to be soaked.)

Start by dumping the beans out onto a tray and sorting through them, throwing away any little pebbles or bits of dirt. Put them in a sieve and rinse them well. Now put them in a large pot and add three times as much water as the beans.

Quick-soak: The quickest way is to bring the water to a boil and boil for a few minutes. Remove from the heat, cover and set it aside to soak for 1 hour.

Overnight soak: Just let the beans and water soak overnight or for at least 8 hours.

2. COOKING THE BEANS

Drain the soaked beans, rinse them, and return them to the pot. Cover with fresh water—twice the amount of water as beans—and bring to a boil. Don't add any salt yet, or they'll take longer to cook.

Reduce the heat, cover, and simmer gently until the beans are tender but not falling apart—unless you like them that way. Most beans will cook in 1 hour to 1½ hours, depending on how fresh they are. Test a bean after 1 hour and if it's not tender, add another ½ cup hot water if needed and continue cooking. Add salt when the beans are just beginning to get tender.

General cooking times: Pinto beans, navy beans, and kidney beans take the longest. Black beans, red beans, and cannellini beans a little less. Lentils and split peas, only about 1 hour (and remember, lentils and split peas don't need to be soaked).

Drain the beans but save the bean broth to use in soups or braises. It's also good to use for cooking rice or other grains.

I hear that it's swampy around New Orleans, but I'm glad you won't find any witches in swamp huts there. So instead of witches making something ominous in their cauldrons, you can prepare this delicious-looking meal. And it's going to be much healthier than what a swamp witch would make!

DIRECTIONS

1. First, soak and cook the beans as directed in How to Cook a Pot of Beans (page 120). Drain and set aside.

2. In a large skillet with a lid or Dutch oven, heat the oil over medium-high heat. Add the sausage and cook and stir for about 3 minutes. Add the onion, bell pepper, and celery and continue cooking and stirring for another few minutes. Add the garlic and cook for another couple of minutes.

3. Add the Cajun seasoning, paprika, broth, tomatoes and their juice, and the drained beans and bring to a boil. Stir in the rice, reduce the heat, cover, and simmer until all the liquid is absorbed and the rice is tender, 15 to 20 minutes. Taste and add salt and pepper if you think it needs it.

4. Let it sit for about 15 minutes before serving.

Ric⟩
in man⟩
the world.⟩
provides a pe⟩
tons of vitamins ⟩
These flavors are fr⟩
Orleans, where the sau⟩
spicy andouille. You could⟩
any sausage you like or keep ⟩
vegetarian without any sausage⟩
at all.

Serves 4 to 6

INGREDIENTS

1/3 pound (2/3 cup) dried red beans

1 tablespoon vegetable or olive oil

3 nice fat sausage links, sliced

1 medium onion, chopped

1 red or green bell pepper, chopped

1 stalk celery, chopped

3 cloves garlic, sliced

2 teaspoons Cajun seasoning

1/2 teaspoon smoked paprika

1 1/2 cups chicken or vegetable broth

1 (14.5-ounce) can diced tomatoes, with their juice

1 cup long-grain white rice

Salt and freshly ground black pepper

ONE-POT RED BEANS AND RICE

...and beans is a dish found
...y cultures around
The combination
...fect protein, with
...and minerals.
...m New
...sage is a
...use

2 bell peppers, ...,
green, chopped

1 small red onion, finely
chopped

1 stalk celery, chopped

1 cup grape or cherry tomatoes,
halved

1 teaspoon dried thyme

3/4 cup Sweet and Spicy Dressing
(recipe follows)

1/4 cup chopped fresh parsley
or basil (or a combination)

...as or charcoal
...he corn on the
...rill, turning
...lly, until charred on
...about 10 minutes.
...ively, do this indoors
...is flame or under a
...Let the corn cool,
...the kernels off with
...knife and put them
...e bowl.

2. Add the bell peppers, onion, celery, tomatoes, and thyme and toss together gently with a large spoon.

3. Stir in the dressing and the chopped herbs and serve at room temperature or chilled.

SWEET AND SPICY DRESSING

Use this dressing on any green salad or to brush on vegetables before roasting or grilling.

Makes 1²⁄₃ cups

INGREDIENTS

1/2 cup apple cider vinegar

1/3 cup sugar

1 clove garlic, grated

2 teaspoons Cajun seasoning

1 cup canola oil

DIRECTIONS

1. In a small bowl, whisk together the vinegar and sugar, whisking until the sugar is dissolved. This should take just a few minutes.

2. Whisk in the garlic and Cajun seasoning. Adding a couple of spoonfuls at a time, whisk in the oil until all the oil is added and the dressing is smooth. The dressing keeps well in the refrigerator for up to 1 week.

PASTA E FAGIOLI

Save the rinds from hunks of parmesan or get them from a cheese shop or Italian grocery if you have one nearby. Remove them before serving. They are also good cold for teething!

Serves 4 to 6

INGREDIENTS

⅓ pound (⅔ cup) dried cannellini beans

2 tablespoons olive oil

1 medium onion, chopped

1 large stalk celery, chopped

2 medium carrots, peeled and chopped

3 cloves garlic, chopped

1 (6-ounce) can tomato paste

1 quart chicken or vegetable broth

1 nice big sprig of fresh basil or 2 teaspoons dried basil

A piece of parmesan rind, if you can get one, plus some grated parmesan for serving

1 cup ditalini or other small pasta shape

Salt and freshly ground black pepper

> You can make this dish in a big bowl, much bigger than bowls where I come from, so it contains lots of servings. I'm jealous, I admit!

DIRECTIONS

1. First, soak and cook the beans as directed in How to Cook a Pot of Beans (page 120). Drain and set aside.

2. In a large saucepan, heat the oil over medium-high heat. Add the onion, celery, carrots, and garlic and cook and stir until the vegetables soften and begin to brown, about 8 minutes.

3. Stir in the tomato paste and cook and stir for another minute.

4. Add the broth, basil, and parmesan rind (if using) and bring to a boil. Stir in the pasta and drained beans and cook until the pasta is tender, about 8 minutes.

5. To serve, remove the rind. Sprinkle the soup with some grated parmesan, as well as salt and pepper to taste.

The next time I need to get healthier after dealing with a wither, I don't want to just drink milk—I want to drink one of these! Not only will I be feeling better in no time, but my taste buds will be so happy too, like I get happy when I open a chest and find a nice ingredient.

HOW TO MAKE A
SMOOTHIE

The difference between a smoothie and a shake is that a smoothie has more fruit/ veggies and no ice cream. If you want to make a smoothie into a shake, replace some of the fruit with a scoop of ice cream.

Serves 2

DIRECTIONS

In a high-powered blender, combine the fruit and/or vegetables, liquid, thickener, sweetener, and ice and blend until smooth.

INGREDIENTS

2 cups cut-up fruit and/or vegetables

1 cup liquid (whey, milk, plant milk, or kefir)

¼ cup thickener (nut butter, Nutella, Greek yogurt, soft pitted dates, oats, cornflakes, or puffed cereal)

A tablespoon or two of sweetener (maple syrup, honey, agave, or fruit preserves)

3 ice cubes

I know about lime dye and the different ways I can craft it, but this recipe has nothing to do with dye. It's about a fruit on Earth called lime, which I see is the same color as our dye. But I don't know if Earth limes would be good for making lime wool to wear.

KEY LIME PIE SMOOTHIE

Tastes EXACTLY like Key lime pie and you won't even know there's avocado in it. Avocado is a fruit, not a vegetable—did you know that?

Serves 2

INGREDIENTS

1 large avocado, halved and pitted

Juice of 4 limes

$1/3$ cup canned sweetened condensed milk

$1/3$ cup whole milk

4 tablespoons store-bought graham cracker crumbs

3 ice cubes

DIRECTIONS

Scoop the avocado flesh into the jar of a blender. (Throw away the pit or plant it in a pot on your windowsill.) Add the lime juice, condensed milk, whole milk, graham cracker crumbs, and ice to the blender and blend until smooth.

EMERALD SMOOTHIE

Serve this in a green sippy cup. You can't taste the spinach in this smoothie, and if you drink it out of a closed green cup, you can't see it, either!

Serves 2

INGREDIENTS

$1 1/2$ cups banana chunks

$1/2$ cup tightly packed baby spinach

1 cup vanilla plant milk

$1/4$ cup soft pitted Medjool dates

3 ice cubes

DIRECTIONS

In a high-powered blender, combine the banana, spinach, milk, dates, and ice and blend until smooth.

PÃO DE QUEIJO

Pão de queijo means "cheese bread" in Portuguese. It's a favorite in Brazil where it's made with tapioca flour (technically a starch) that comes from the pulp of the yuca root (aka cassava root). These small breads are crispy on the outside and soft and cheesy on the inside—and naturally gluten free!

Makes 12

INGREDIENTS

Cooking spray
1 cup whole milk
½ cup vegetable oil
2 cups tapioca flour
1 teaspoon salt
2 large eggs
1 cup grated parmesan cheese

And I thought bread made with potatoes was impressive! I'd never even heard of tapioca. Is there anything you can't make bread out of?

DIRECTIONS

1. Preheat the oven to 375°F. Lightly grease 12 cups of a muffin tin with cooking spray.

2. In a blender, combine the milk, oil, tapioca flour, salt, eggs, and parmesan and blend until smooth. Scrape down the sides of the jar to make sure all the flour gets mixed in.

3. Divide the batter evenly among the prepared muffin cups and transfer to the oven.

4. Bake until puffed and golden, 25 to 30 minutes. You can either serve them warm or remove the breads from the pan, place them on a wire rack, and let them cool completely.

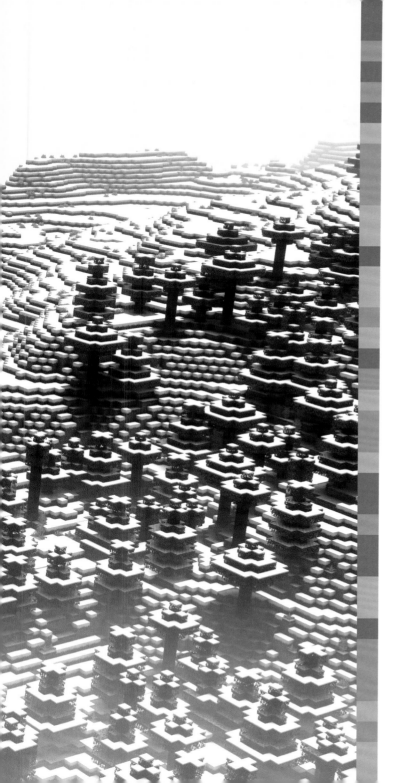

TAIGAS

In Alaska, Russia, northern Europe, Greenland, and other northernmost parts of the world, you can find one of Earth's coldest biomes: the taiga. Chilly winds sweep through the pine forests of this landscape, and vegetation hunkers close to the acidic soil.

To the north of the taiga biome, you'll find tundra—treeless plains with nutrient-poor soil. Dig down there through the thin layer that thaws during the summer and you'll hit permafrost—a permanent layer of frozen earth. The earth is often wet and boggy, but at the same time, tundras often get less rain than some deserts. Doesn't sound very pleasant, does it?

To the plants and animals that live there, the taiga is home. They all have special adaptations to help them survive long, dark, cold winters and short summers. The pine trees have very little sap, so there's less to freeze. And their needles have three sides—all the better to absorb as much sun as they can! Plants like mosses grow close to the ground and in clumps to help them avoid the wind that screams across the soil, threatening to unearth their roots.

I love the cold weather and snow that the taiga can get. Sliding on ice is so fun! And who doesn't love a snowball?

Because they are low down, the snow that falls in the winter insulates them. Taiga mammals know how to handle this cold biome as well. Mammals like lemmings, arctic foxes, hares, and caribou grow thick fur and layers of fat to insulate them against the cold. In the winter, some animals' fur turns white for better camouflage against the snow. And they make the most of the brief summers by breeding and raising their babies quickly, before long, dark winter sets in again.

For all its frozen toughness, the taiga is under threat from clear-cutting and deforestation. When people cut down the needle trees for lumber or warmth, the roots that held the soil in place decay. The soil loosens and blows away.

The taiga and the tundra are deeply affected by climate change also. As the temperature on the planet goes up, the permafrost is becoming much less permanent. In fact, it's thawing, and as it does, it releases the greenhouse gases carbon dioxide and methane, which then further add to the climate change burden our planet is carrying. Then temperatures keep rising and—*boom*—more thawing.

And when the soil warms up, other plants are suddenly able to grow in these biomes that were previously too cold for them. This might sound just fine—who doesn't like plants?—but the caribou and other Arctic animals might feel differently. They've evolved to eat certain taiga and tundra plants, and when other plants take over, then they lose their food source. Parasites can also live in these new, warmer biomes now and feed on the Arctic animals, transmitting diseases.

Controlling the warming of the planet will save the taiga biome. This seems like a huge, overwhelming job! How could one person's actions make any difference in the pool of carbon we're all swimming in?

It does.

Committing to electric cars, asking for clean energy like wind and solar instead of coal and natural gas, buying from companies that support climate change solutions, and supporting officials who promote carbon reduction does make a difference. You can talk to the adults in your life about these efforts. The planet's delicate northern taiga needs you—and you can help it.

HOW YOU CAN HELP

Creating refuges and protected areas for the taiga and tundra's plants and animals is another way we can protect these delicate biomes. You can't create a wildlife refuge by yourself, but you can support governments and organizations who are.

Do a google search to find out what's already being done to protect cold biome animals. Try search words like "taiga," "tundra," "protection," "wildlife," and "refuge."

Once you find an effort that's underway, do some reading to find out if an organization is working to create or support a refuge, or if the movement is being led by a federal, local, or indigenous government. If an organization is leading the effort, do a quick internet search on that organization. Look them up on an evaluating website like Charity Navigator. You want to make sure that any nonprofit you're supporting is using money carefully and honestly.

Then, examine what the group or government is trying to do. Is there a law they are working to get passed? If so, write an email or a letter of support to the government official in charge. Are they looking for funds to support their work? Then see if you can get donations from your friends or the adults in your life. Do they need helpers? Perhaps there's a local event you can volunteer for.

Tell others in your life what you're doing and why protecting the taiga and the tundra from climate change is important. You might find that they want to help as well.

The polar bears in Minecraft like it cold, and so do the polar bears on Earth. Let's make sure both kinds of polar bears can keep chilling! You might be able to get your parents or teachers involved in taking better care of the planet so we will always have polar bears both in my world and yours.

HOW TO MAKE
FRUIT ICES

There are many kinds of iced desserts: Italian ice, sorbet, granita, shave ice, and snow cones, to name a few. All but ices and granita require special equipment to process.

Serves 4

INGREDIENTS

½ cup sugar

1 cup water

3 cups fruit juice (pomegranate and grape are good)

1 tablespoon fresh lemon juice

DIRECTIONS

1. In a saucepan over medium-high heat, stir together the sugar and water. Bring to a boil, stirring until the sugar dissolves. Cool completely.

2. Once cooled, stir in the fruit juice and lemon juice. Pour into a 9 × 13-inch metal baking pan.

3. Place in the freezer to freeze. Every 30 minutes, stir with a fork to break up the ice crystals. It should take 3 to 4 hours for the ice to become frozen and fluffy.

Fruit ices are icy like the ice spikes biome, though they taste a lot better than ice or snow! When I see ice in Minecraft, I might take my pickaxe to break it. For fruit ices, you can just take a spoon to scoop it up and guide it into your mouth!

VARIATION

Lemon Ice: Follow the recipe for Basic Fruit Ice with these changes: Increase the sugar to 1 cup. For the liquids use 3½ cups water and 1 cup fresh lemon juice (from 4 to 5 lemons).

CHOCOLATE MILK GRANITA

Granita is an Italian ice made by the same method as the basic Fruit Ice except you break up the ice so the texture becomes flaky and light and a little crunchier.

In other words, don't take a pickaxe to this granita!

INGREDIENT

1 quart chocolate milk

DIRECTIONS

1. Pour the chocolate milk into a 9 × 13-inch metal baking pan.

2. Place in the freezer and freeze for 30 minutes.

3. Scrape the partially frozen bits with the tines of a fork and refreeze. Do this every 30 minutes until the granita becomes frozen and flaky. This will take 3 to 4 hours.

HOW TO MAKE
MEATBALLS

Dipping your hands in cold water keeps the meat from sticking to them. Roll the balls loosely; too tightly packed and the meatballs will become tough.

Serves 4 to 6

INGREDIENTS

Cooking spray

1 medium onion, grated

2 fat cloves garlic, grated

½ cup plain dried bread crumbs

3 tablespoons milk or broth

2 large eggs

1 teaspoon salt

½ teaspoon freshly ground black pepper

2 pounds ground meat (beef, pork, turkey, chicken, or lamb, or a combination)

Marinara or barbecue sauce (optional)

Drinks like chocolate milk granitas and fruit ices give the cold feel of the taiga, but if you're actually living someplace cold, it's usually nice to warm up with a hot meal. This recipe will keep you toasty on the coldest of days. If I were to make this recipe in Minecraft, though, I wouldn't make meatballs. . . . I'd make meatblocks!

DIRECTIONS

1. Preheat the oven to 400°F. Lightly grease a baking sheet with cooking spray.

2. In a large bowl, combine the onion, garlic, bread crumbs, milk, eggs, salt, and pepper. Add the meat and mix only until everything is combined. Don't overmix or the meatballs will be tough.

3. Fill a bowl with cold water. Dip your hands in the cold water (this prevents the meat from sticking) and loosely roll a walnut-size amount of meat into a ball. Place it on the prepared baking sheet and continue until all the meatballs are formed.

4. Bake the meatballs until no longer pink inside, 15 to 20 minutes.

5. If you'd like, transfer them to a skillet and heat them up in simmering marinara or barbecue sauce.

The spices added to this recipe give it a really unique flavor. For some reason, a freshly-cooked Swedish meatball makes me feel all warm and fuzzy. Almost like a memory from your hometown, reminding you of the place you were born and raised... I wonder why.

SWEDISH MEATBALLS

Serves 4 to 6

INGREDIENTS

Cooking spray

Basic meatballs mixture (opposite), with changes (see step 2)

1 teaspoon freshly grated nutmeg

1/2 teaspoon ground cardamom

1/2 cup sour cream

Salt and freshly ground black pepper

GRAVY

4 tablespoons butter

4 tablespoons all-purpose flour

3 cups beef broth

DIRECTIONS

1. Preheat the oven to 400°F. Lightly grease a baking sheet with cooking spray.

2. Make the basic meatball mixture with these changes: Omit the garlic. Add the nutmeg and cardamom when adding the salt and pepper. Use half pork and half beef.

3. Form the mixture into balls the size of a walnut, arrange on the prepared baking sheet, and bake until no longer pink inside, 15 to 20 minutes.

4. Meanwhile, make the gravy: In a large skillet, melt the butter over medium heat. Whisk in the flour—this is called a roux (pronounced ROO)—and cook and stir until the roux becomes a nut brown. Whisk in the broth, about 1 cup at a time, until the gravy is smooth and bubbling. Reduce the heat and keep warm until the meatballs are done.

5. Add the meatballs to the gravy and heat through, about 5 minutes.

6. Just before serving, season with a little salt and pepper. Carefully stir in the sour cream.

KOTLETA

These are Eastern European meatballs made with chicken, mushrooms, and carrots. They're made with the same basic meatball recipe but formed into chubby little ovals.

Serves 4 to 6

INGREDIENTS

Cooking spray

4 tablespoons butter

8 large mushrooms, finely chopped

1 medium carrot, peeled and grated

1 teaspoon freshly ground black pepper

Basic meatballs mixture (page 140) made with ground dark meat chicken

I can vouch for how good mushrooms and carrots are. I can see why people in Ukraine, Poland, and Russia really like to eat this dish. Even when it's snowing outside, you can sit by your fireplace and eat up while you heat up!

DIRECTIONS

1. Preheat the oven to 400°F. Lightly grease a baking sheet with cooking spray.

2. In a skillet, melt 2 tablespoons of the butter over medium-high heat. Add the mushrooms and carrots and cook until softened and beginning to brown, about 5 minutes. Add the pepper and stir. Remove from the pan to a plate to cool completely. Melt the remaining 2 tablespoons butter in the skillet (no need to wash it) and set aside.

3. Put together the meatball mixture as directed in the basic meatball recipe, adding the cooled mushrooms and carrots along with the onion and garlic. Form the mixture into 12 slightly flattened ovals and place on the prepared baking sheet. Brush with the melted butter.

4. Bake until no longer pink inside, 25 to 30 minutes.

CARDAMOM BEAR PAWS

Cardamom is a favorite spice in Scandinavia, where it's used in cakes, cookies, and breads.

Makes 8

INGREDIENTS

Potato Bread dough (page 20)

FILLING

1 stick (4 ounces) butter, at room temperature

1½ cups powdered sugar

2 egg whites

2 teaspoons ground cardamom

½ teaspoon ground cinnamon

2½ cups almond flour, plus more for dusting

TOPPING

1 large egg

½ cup sliced almonds

GLAZE

1 cup powdered sugar

3 tablespoons milk

1 teaspoon vanilla extract

Why would anyone want to eat a claw from a polar bear or panda bear? Oh, wait, this is just a dessert food that's shaped like bear paws! Polar bears can be found in icy parts of my world, and when I see them, I stay back and give them enough space to know I won't bother them, especially when they have cubs. But I can't stay away from this dessert.

DIRECTIONS

1. Make the potato bread dough and let it rise once (through step 5), then refrigerate while you make the filling.

2. **Make the filling:** In a large bowl, using a wooden spoon (or an electric mixer), combine the butter and ¾ cup of the powdered sugar and beat to combine. Beat in the egg whites, the remaining ¾ cup powdered sugar, cardamom, cinnamon, and almond flour. Cover and refrigerate until you're ready to use it.

3. Line two baking sheets with silicone baking mats.

4. **Prepare the topping:** Separate the egg into two small bowls. Add 1 tablespoon water to the yolk and stir with a fork. This is the egg wash. Set the sliced almonds and egg white aside for later.

5. Dump the dough out onto a lightly floured work surface and divide into 2 equal portions. Working with half of the dough at a time, roll it out into a thin rectangle about 14 × 4 inches. Spread half of the filling down the middle of the dough (lengthwise). Brush half of the egg wash along one of the long edges and fold the long sides together, over the filling. Press the edges to make sure it's sealed.

6. Cut the roll crosswise into 4 pieces about 3½ inches long. Make 4 parallel slits into the folded edge of each "paw" and curve the paw so the slits separate into "claws." Put them on one of the prepared baking sheets, leaving plenty of space between them. Repeat the process with the other half of the dough and the remaining filling and egg wash.

7. Loosely cover the paws with a paper towel and let them rise for about 30 minutes while you preheat the oven to 350°F.

8. Brush the paws with the egg white and sprinkle with the almond slices. Transfer to the oven and bake until puffed and golden brown, 25 to 30 minutes.

9. Remove from the oven and let cool completely before glazing.

10. **Meanwhile, make the glaze:** In a small bowl, whisk the powdered sugar, milk, and vanilla together until smooth and creamy.

11. Drizzle the glaze over the cooled bear paws.

THE END

The ends of the Earth! The ends of the Earth? The place is a sphere, so there's no beginning and no end. Humans have mapped the globe, so we know there're no mythic lands full of dragons and monsters.

But that doesn't mean that all of Earth's mysteries are known to us. Below the crust of soil and sand and rock and grass, below the heaving waves of the ocean, fire and lava rumble and roil. There, superheated rock melts into magma. Volcanoes thrust up from trenches miles deep. Caverns twist and turn, sparkling with crystals, while blind cave crickets scurry by. Cold, dark, deep, hot—the Earth's extreme places are waiting for us to explore.

On your old maps, they used to write "here there be dragons" over dangerous, unexplored places.

You might not have an actual dragon lurking in your world's End, but the experiences there sound just as thrilling!

AMAZING FACTS ABOUT EARTH'S MOST EXTREME PLACES

- The deepest known spot on Earth is the Mariana Trench, 1,500 miles long and seven miles deep—just under 37,000 feet. For comparison, whales don't usually dive below 8,200 feet. The water pressure in the Trench is one thousand times heavier than on land. Challenger Deep, the deepest part of the trench, is 36,070 feet below sea level. Only three people, encased in deep-sea submersibles, have ever been down to the bottom. A person diving to the bottom of the Mariana Trench must travel in a submersible—the water pressure is too heavy without one. Crustaceans and fish that live in the Mariana Trench are specially adapted to the cold and dark.

- Volcanoes give us a glimpse of the insides of the Earth—a boiling, roiling, steaming glimpse. Magma, the molten rock inside a volcano, can reach between 1,200° and 2,300°F. Once it erupts from the volcano in the form of lava, it's able to melt everything it touches. Volcanoes release a huge amount of energy during an eruption. When a volcano in Southeast Asia erupted in the late nineteenth century, it released enough energy to match 15,000 nuclear bombs. One of the world's largest volcanic eruptions happened in 1912 in Alaska. The volcano Novarupta erupted for three days and released fifteen cubic kilometers of lava—sixty times the amount released by the volcano Mount Saint Helens seventy years later. It caused earthquakes for five days before the eruption and released an ash cloud that stretched one hundred miles from the volcano.

- Deep under the surface of the Earth, caves form when rain and carbon dioxide mix and seep into rock like limestone, dolomite, and gypsum. The rock under the ground slowly dissolves, making a hole. It can take 100,000 years for a cave to widen enough to hold a human. Stalactites and stalagmites are made from dripping water, while other formations look like mushrooms, twisty straws, or sheets of flowing rock. Under the rolling bluegrass of Kentucky lies the world's longest known cave system, Mammoth Cave. Four hundred miles have been explored by scientists, who estimate that another six hundred are still unexplored.

HOW YOU CAN HELP

You don't need to go to the ends of the Earth—or deep beneath its surface—to help our planet. Instead, you can find challenges inside the screen of your laptop, inside the walls of your home, or out on the streets.

- **Organize a boycott.** A lot of private companies have a big role in contributing to climate change and pollution. Calling out companies publicly and refusing to use their products can make them sit up and listen. Once you've identified a company whose climate and sustainability policies could use some cleanup, write up a list of what you want to see the company change. Then recruit as many people as you can—social media is great for this. Everyone makes a pledge not to use the company's products, whatever they are, until the company agrees to some of the changes. Then—and this is key—make your boycott public. Post on social media, so everyone knows what you're doing. Are you able to call your local news stations and newspapers? A lot of people get their information that way. Let the reporters know which company you're boycotting and why. Tell all your fellow boycotters to do the same thing.

- **Make a pledge to go plastic-free.** Pick a certain time period—a day, a week, a month—and try to avoid using or buying products made with plastic. Then make sure lots of other people know what you're doing. Explain your pledge on social media or at your school, with permission. Then update people regularly on how your awareness campaign is going.

- **Protest.** Your face and your voice are powerful tools. Do you see something you know is hurting the natural areas in your community? Are issues coming up in your local government that support or harm sustainability around you? Do some research to learn as much as you can about the issue. Then break out the poster board and markers. Make yourself a sign saying what you think is right or wrong about the issue. Gather some friends, gather some more signs, then hit the streets. Hold your sign up high and say what you think—chanting, singing, or any other way. Stay respectful, of course, and calm—but persistent.

This chapter is going to take a lot of what we've learned together in the rest of our adventure, and show us new ways to use it. Just like in Minecraft, your experience traveling the other biomes will give you the tools you need to tackle the End's challenges!

COCONUT TRES LECHES CAKE

Tres leches means "three milks" in Spanish and is also the name of a cake that's made in many Latin American countries. This one should really be called Cinco Leches—Five Milks: 1) There is buttermilk in the cake batter. 2, 3, and 4) The finished cake is soaked in coconut milk, evaporated milk, and sweetened condensed milk. 5) The cake is topped with whipped cream!

Makes one 9 × 13-inch cake

INGREDIENTS

CAKE

2 sticks (8 ounces) butter, melted

2½ cups all-purpose flour

2 teaspoons baking powder

½ teaspoon baking soda

½ teaspoon salt

1½ cups granulated sugar

4 large eggs

1 teaspoon vanilla or coconut extract

1¼ cups whey or buttermilk

> I've only ever known one kind of milk, so working with five different kinds of milk (and I don't think it's just because you get it from five different cows) is really going to be a treat. I can't wait to taste how the coconut's sweet tropical flavor will add to the cake.

DIRECTIONS

1. **Make the cake:** Preheat the oven to 350°F. Grease a 9 × 13-inch cake pan by brushing it with a thin layer of the melted butter.

2. In a small bowl, stir together the flour, baking powder, baking soda, and salt.

3. In a large bowl, using an electric mixer, beat the melted butter and granulated sugar until light and fluffy. Beat in the eggs, one at a time. Beat in the extract and half of the whey. Beat in half of the flour mixture, then the rest of the whey, then the rest of the flour mixture.

4. Scrape the batter into the prepared cake pan and bake until a toothpick inserted in the center comes out clean, 25 to 30 minutes.

5. Let the cake cool completely in the pan.

6. **Make the milk soak:** In a large spouted measuring cup or pitcher, combine the coconut milk, evaporated milk, condensed milk, and vanilla.

7. Once the cake has cooled, use a toothpick or a skewer to poke small holes all over the cake all the way through to the bottom. Pour the milk mixture over the cake, covering it entirely. Don't worry if it seems to be a lot; the cake will soak up all the milk as it sits.

8. Cover the cake and refrigerate for at least 3 hours or up to 24 hours.

9. **Make the topping:** In a bowl, using an electric mixer, combine the cream, vanilla, and powdered sugar and beat until stiff peaks form.

10. Spread the topping over the cake and sprinkle with cinnamon before serving.

INGREDIENTS (CONT.)

MILK SOAK

1 (13.5-ounce) can coconut milk

1 (5-ounce) can evaporated milk

1 (14-ounce) can sweetened condensed milk

1 teaspoon vanilla extract

TOPPING

$1\frac{1}{2}$ cups heavy whipping cream

$\frac{1}{2}$ teaspoon vanilla extract

$\frac{1}{3}$ cup powdered sugar

Cinnamon, for sprinkling

1,2,3 YOGURT CAKE

This is a cake that uses little yogurt containers to measure some of the ingredients. If you've made your own yogurt, just use a ½-cup measure.

Makes one 8-inch round cake

INGREDIENTS

Cooking spray

1 (4- or 5-ounce) container plain yogurt or ½ cup yogurt

3 yogurt containers of all-purpose flour

1 teaspoon baking powder

3 large eggs

2 yogurt containers of sugar

1 teaspoon vanilla extract

1 yogurt container of vegetable or olive oil

Grated zest of ½ lemon or orange

Milk or berries and cream, for serving

This brings back the yogurt I learned to love in the desert section and adds a cake aspect to it. If you want to add a candle or more to it to make it more Minecraft-y, that's up to you.

DIRECTIONS

1. Preheat the oven to 350°F. Grease an 8-inch round cake pan with cooking spray.

2. Empty the yogurt into a large bowl. Wash and dry the container and use it to measure the other ingredients.

3. In a medium bowl, mix the flour and baking powder.

4. Add the eggs, sugar, and vanilla to the yogurt and whisk well. Whisk in the oil and lemon zest. Very gently, add the flour mixture to the yogurt mixture and mix gently just to combine. Don't overmix or it will become rubbery!

5. Pour the batter into the prepared pan and bake until a toothpick or skewer inserted in the center of the cake comes out clean, 25 to 35 minutes.

6. Let it cool for 10 minutes in the pan, then remove from the pan and set on a wire rack to cool completely. Serve with milk for dunking, or with berries and cream.

BEANY BUTTER BROWNIES

There's no gluten in this! Beans have enough starch to act as a binder and they disappear into these fudgy, chewy, chocolate and peanut butter brownies. Tons of protein, too!

Makes 12 brownies

INGREDIENTS

Cooking spray

1 (15-ounce) can black or red beans, drained, or 2 cups cooked beans

3 large eggs

2 tablespoons creamy peanut butter

3 tablespoons butter, melted

1 teaspoon vanilla extract

1/3 cup packed light brown sugar

1/3 cup granulated sugar

1/4 cup unsweetened cocoa powder

1/2 teaspoon salt

1/2 teaspoon baking powder

1/2 cup chocolate chips or chopped chocolate from a bar

There are plenty of things in Minecraft that are the color brown. Dirt, trees, or dye made from cocoa beans. And come to think of it, many of my favorite foods are, too: steak, mutton, or mushroom stew. I can't wait to add this food to the list.

Would chocolate make a good brown dye? I'm too busy eating it to find out.

DIRECTIONS

1. Preheat the oven to 350°F. Grease an 8-inch square cake pan with cooking spray.

2. In a microwave, cook the beans for 30 seconds.

3. In a food processor, combine the warmed beans and 1 of the eggs and puree until it's as smooth as possible. Scrape this into a large bowl.

4. One at a time, whisk in the remaining 2 eggs, the peanut butter, melted butter, and vanilla. Whisk in both of the sugars.

5. In a separate bowl, sift together the cocoa, salt, and baking powder. Add the flour mixture to the bean mixture, mixing until smooth. Stir in the chocolate bits. Scrape the batter into the prepared pan.

6. Bake until you can shake the pan without it jiggling, 25 to 30 minutes. Cool completely in the pan before cutting into 12 brownies.

What's this about adding spice to pumpkin? Hmm, you take pumpkin puree for this, which is a little different from taking a sword and whacking a pumpkin open. Once it's in puree form you can't put it on your head (or if you do, you'll probably regret it), but it does make it easier to mix other sweet things in with it.

PUMPKIN SPICE LATTE CAKES

There's no milk or coffee in these, but baked in mugs and topped with white chocolate ganache, they sure look like a PSL.

Makes 4 mug cakes

INGREDIENTS

Cooking spray
2 large eggs
1/2 cup packed light brown sugar
1/2 cup granulated sugar
1/2 cup canola oil
1 cup canned unsweetened pumpkin puree
2 teaspoons pumpkin pie spice
1 teaspoon vanilla extract
1 cup all-purpose flour
1 teaspoon baking powder
1 teaspoon baking soda
1/2 teaspoon salt

WHITE CHOCOLATE GANACHE
1 cup white chocolate chips
8 tablespoons heavy cream

DIRECTIONS

1. Preheat the oven to 350°F. Grease four ovenproof coffee mugs with cooking spray.

2. In a large bowl, whisk together the eggs, brown sugar, and granulated sugar. Beat in the oil, pumpkin puree, pumpkin pie spice, and vanilla.

3. In a separate bowl, stir together the flour, baking powder, baking soda, and salt. Add the flour mixture to the pumpkin mixture and whisk gently to combine. Do not overmix!

4. Divide the batter evenly among the prepared mugs and bake until a toothpick or skewer inserted into the center of one comes out clean, 20 to 25 minutes.

5. Let the cakes cool completely in the mugs.

6. **Meanwhile, make the white chocolate ganache:** In a small microwave-safe bowl, mix the white chocolate chips and cream and microwave in 15-second increments, stirring well after each until melted. Let the mixture cool at room temperature to spreading consistency, about 1 hour—or in the fridge, about 20 minutes.

7. Frost the mug cakes with the white chocolate ganache.

COMPOST TRUFFLES

A cross between a chocolate truffle and an energy bite.

Makes 24 truffles

INGREDIENTS

1 cup semisweet chocolate chips

¾ cup heavy cream

1 cup chopped dried fruit (dates, raisins, figs, apples, pears, or mango)

2 cups crushed crispy cereal (crispy rice, cornflakes, or oat rings), crushed

1 cup crushed salty snacks (potato chips, sweet potato chips, or pretzels)

1 cup finely chopped toasted nuts

Don't worry, you're not really eating compost here. It's just made to look like compost. As little snack bites, these could be good to carry around and share with your friends.

DIRECTIONS

1. In a small microwave-safe bowl, mix the chocolate chips and cream and microwave in 15-second increments, stirring well after each until melted. Scrape the chocolate ganache into a larger bowl (big enough to hold the other ingredients) and let cool at room temperature to spreading consistency, about 1 hour—or in the fridge, about 20 minutes.

2. Add the dried fruit, cereal, and salty snacks to the ganache and stir together until evenly mixed. Refrigerate until firm, about 30 minutes.

3. Put the chopped nuts in a shallow bowl. Line a baking sheet with parchment paper or a silicone baking mat.

4. Scoop out a spoonful of ganache mixture and roll it into a 1½-inch ball. Roll the truffle in the nuts and place on the prepared baking sheet. Continue with the rest of the truffles. If they begin to get too soft, return them to the fridge.

5. Store them in the fridge in an airtight container for up to 2 weeks.

Hello again, potato bread! Taking recipes you've already learned and using them as components for something new is a lot like crafting, isn't it? Multiple stages for one amazing result.

CINNAMON SUGAR ZEPPOLE

Fried dough is in almost every culture, whether they're called zeppole, fritters, beignets, bomboloni, or donuts. These are made with our basic potato bread recipe.

Makes about 24 zeppole

INGREDIENTS

Potato Bread dough (page 20) with changes (see step 1)
¼ cup cinnamon sugar
½ cup powdered sugar
Canola oil or coconut oil, for frying

DIRECTIONS

1. Make the potato bread dough with these changes: Increase the granulated sugar to ⅓ cup and add grated lemon (or orange) zest (from 1 lemon or orange) and 2 teaspoons vanilla extract when adding the eggs. Let the dough rise once (through step 5).

2. Place the cinnamon sugar and the powdered sugar in separate paper lunch bags.

3. Rub a baking sheet with a little bit of oil. Line a second baking sheet with paper towels. Pour 2 inches of oil into a heavy-bottomed pot and heat to 375°F on a deep-fry thermometer.

4. Grab a walnut-sized piece of dough, pull it up, and, making an "o" with your thumb and forefinger, squeeze it until the little piece pops off. Drop it onto the oiled baking sheet. Continue until all the dough is used.

5. Carefully put a few zeppole on a large, slotted spoon and lower them into the oil. You can fry several at a time, just not so many that they crowd the pot. Cook them for a few minutes on each side, until they puff up and brown. Remove them to the paper towels to drain. While they're still warm, shake them in the bag of either powdered or cinnamon sugar.

CONCLUSION

This has been quite an adventure for me. I've come a long way since my days where a typical meal consisted of a porkchop, carrots, and a pumpkin pie. Back then I could go to bed while the zombies groaned outside my door and immediately wake up to the next morning, dreaming of the potato I would have for breakfast. But there's so much more out there, now. I want to experience it all!

I hope you've enjoyed learning about the world and its delicious meals as much as I have. You're so lucky to have so many astonishing places to see and foods to enjoy. I come from a place of enchanted treasure and fantastical mobs, sure. But I think Earth might be even more magical than the Overworld.

But as amazing as it is, the planet needs your help. And I also hope that this book has inspired you to take action, and that it's given you some first steps. Because here's a similarity between your world and mine: You have all the tools you need to make a safe and beautiful home, for you and all your friends to live in. All you have to do is get crafting.

I'm heading back to Minecraft now. I wish I could bring it all back with me, but that won't work. I guess I'll just have to visit you again sometime very soon! Maybe you'll run in to me while you're playing a game! I'll be working in my garden or at my kitchen, seeing what new recipes I can try.

INDEX

ABOUT THE AUTHOR

EMMA CARLSON BERNE is a children's author who often writes about sustainability and the natural world. Her other books include *The Wizard of Oz Cookbook*, *The Ultimate Driving Book*, and *Star Wars: Forces of Destiny*. She also writes mysteries and historical fiction for American Girl, PJ Library, and Little Passports. Emma lives in Cincinnati with her husband, their two cats, and their three boys who loved helping her understand the intricacies of Minecraft for this book. More on Emma can be found at emmacarlsonberne.com.

DANICA DAVIDSON is the critically acclaimed author of nineteen books for young readers, including twelve unofficial Minecraft novels, manga art books, and the middle-grade Holocaust memoir *I Will Protect You*, which she wrote with survivor Eva Mozes Kor. Davidson loves her dogs and cats, anime, and swinging on her swing while thinking up stories.

VICTORIA GRANOF is a food creative—director, stylist, author, and recipe developer—who lives in the biome of Brooklyn with her Minecraft-obsessed son, Theo, who taught her everything she knows about beating the Ender Dragon! She is currently working on a book about Sicilian pastries.

Copyright © 2024 Mojang AB. All rights reserved. Minecraft, the Minecraft logo, the Mojang Studios logo, and the Creeper logo are trademarks of the Microsoft group of companies.

All rights reserved.

Published in the United States by Random House Worlds, an imprint of Random House, a division of Penguin Random House LLC, New York.
RandomHouseBooks.com

RANDOM HOUSE is a registered trademark, and RANDOM HOUSE WORLDS and colophon are trademarks of Penguin Random House LLC.

ISBN 978-0-593-57992-3
Ebook ISBN 978-0-593-57993-0

Library of Congress Cataloging-in-Publication Data

Names: Granof, Victoria, 1958- author. | Bernay, Emma, 1979- author. | Davidson, Danica, author.
Title: Minecraft : the crafter's kitchen : an official cookbook for young chefs and their families / Victoria Granof, Emma Bernay, Danica Davidson.
Description: First edition. | New York : Penguin Random House, [2023] | Includes index. | Audience: Grades 4-6
Identifiers: LCCN 2023030636 (print) | LCCN 2023030637 (ebook) | ISBN 9780593579923 (hardcover) | ISBN 9780593579930 (ebook)
Subjects: LCSH: Cooking—Technique—Juvenile literature. | Baking—Technique—Juvenile literature. | LCGFT: Cookbooks.
Classification: LCC TX652.5 G7125 2023 (print) | LCC TX652.5 (ebook) | DDC 641.3—dc23/eng/20230714

LC record available at https://lccn.loc.gov/2023030636

LC ebook record available at https://lccn.loc.gov/2023030637

Printed in China

Editor: Alex Davis
Production editor: Natalie Blachere
Editorial assistant: Lydia Estrada
Art director: Ian Dingman
Designer: Jan Derevjanik
Mojang: Kelsey Ranallo, Jay Castello, Sherin Kwan, Alex Wiltshire, and Milo Bengtsson
Photographer: Nivi Shaham
Prop stylist: Andrea Greco
Food stylist: Victoria Granof
Prop stylist assistants: Todd Henry, Ashleigh Sarbone
Food stylist assistant: Shannon Dowling
First assistant: Sam Schmieg
Production manager: Kim Tyner
Compositor: Hannah Hunt
Copyeditor: Kate Slate
Proofreaders: Liana Faughnan and Marlene Tungseth
Indexer: Jay Kreider

1 2 3 4 5 6 7 8 9

$PrintCode

First Edition